THE WITCHES OF OZ
by Matthew and Julia Phillips

First published in Australia in 1991

Chapter 6: The 1
written in collaboratio

£4-50

£

THE WITCHES
OF OZ

©1994 Matthew & Julia Phillips

ALL RIGHTS RESERVED

Published by:

Capall Bann Publishing
Freshfields
Chieveley
Berks
RG16 8TF

DEDICATIONS

No book is ever written simply by its author, or authors. More than most, this book owes a great deal to those many people who have taught us, inspired us, encouraged us, and supported us. To all of those people - thank you.

To Rufus - without whom it would not be!

To Miranda, Paul, Marion, Sharon, Elaine, Michaela, JD, Diana, Spencer, Alex, Steve, Sioux,

To Seldiy and Nigel, Jim, Alan, Sophia, Tessa and Graham, Ken, Chris and Smoss, Mike and Linda, Prudence, Wendy, Dave and Sue, Jackie, Maxine and Vincent, Stewart and Janet, Vivianne and Chris, Dave and Debby, Claire, Sandy, Tina and John, Maureen, Murry, Jeremy, Chris and Janet.

To Jenny and Laurence, Nikki, Klaus, Tracey, Kattrina and Steve, Barb, Craig, and Judy.

To Rowan and Russell, Richard and Tamarra, Carol, Michael, Rhea and Raven, Bill and Antonia, Janeena, Martin, Bill and Naomi, Michelle and Padraig, Patricia, Martin, Anna, Alan and Leone, Rob and Janet, James, Nicole, Jill, Trevor, Malcolm, Bridgit and Gawain, Sonya, Michelin and Ken.

And to the future.

Front Cover artwork by Hawkeye
Frontispiece artwork by Hawthorn
Cover design by Daryth Bastin

CONTENTS

Contents

CHAPTER ONE

WHAT IS WICCA?

There is an enormous amount of information which confronts the would-be Wiccan. Knowing where to start, and what books are going to be of the most practical use is the biggest problem which beginners face. Another major problem is finding out what Wicca actually is! This is a question we are often asked, and one which has a fairly simple answer: Wicca is a Pagan religion.

Just as Christians or Muslims are divided into various different sects, so too are Pagans. Some Pagans worship in a formal, structured sense; others are rather more simple in their approach, and may simply meditate quietly, thinking about the Earth, and the turning of the seasons, often expressed through the relationship of the God and Goddess with each other, and with humanity. Some see Paganism as the religious expression of Green Politics without being specific about the worship of a deity, or group of deities. All Pagans, whatever their form of worship, try to attune themselves to the natural order of the Earth, and live in harmony with nature, not contrary, or indifferent to it.

Wicca is a specific tradition within the broader expanse of Paganism in much the same way as Catholic is a specific tradition within the broader expanse of Christianity. Although "Wicca" and "Witchcraft" are not quite the same thing, the words are often used interchangeably, and the distinctions are gradually being eroded. A detailed discussion of the semantics of Wicca and Witchcraft falls outside the scope of this book, but we will have to examine the topic briefly, as it is important.

Witchcraft is an emotive word, and can mean many things. It can be used to describe the local village wise man or woman who heals the sick; it can also be used to describe anyone who curses his or her neighbours! Over a period of several hundreds of years, the Christian Church prosecuted many people in Europe on charges of heresy, which included the practice of Witchcraft. The Christians described the Witches' God as the Devil or Satan - the adversary of their God. Of course this was completely untrue, but for hundreds of years the Witches were accused of devil worship, and regrettably, that belief persists to the present day in some cases. The respect which Witches gave to the Goddess was either subsumed into Christian theology (as with the Virgin Mary, and many Christian "saints"), or suppressed completely.

Wicca, although obviously very closely related to Witchcraft, is generally used to refer to a religion which draws its inspiration from the earliest Pagan religions, but was formalised rather more recently (in the 20th century). It has two main traditions: Gardnerian and Alexandrian. There are others, particularly in the United States, but this book is concerned mainly with practices found in these two main branches.

Gardnerians derive their name from the founder of modern Wicca, Gerald Gardner. He either created, or discovered, (depending on your viewpoint) Wicca in the 1930s/1940s, and initiated a number of people who have continued the tradition in an unbroken line to the present day. Alexandrians derive their name from Alex Sanders, who was initiated into a Gardnerian group in the 1960s, and then developed his own tradition after breaking away from his original group. As time goes by, the two strands are merging, and there are a number of groups now (like our own) which are a combination of Alexandrian and Gardnerian traditions.

Wiccans are followers of a Pagan religion, and see divinity expressed in every part of the universe. The Earth, the planets, the stars, the void: all are part of one great divine source to the Pagan. Many religions teach that divinity is separate from humanity, and from the world in which we live. Wiccans believe that divinity is present everywhere - in our selves, in animals, plants, rocks, the oceans - and can be easily seen in the phases of the Moon, and in the changing seasons. Divinity can be seen in birth and death; in summer and winter; autumn and spring; in men and women; boys and girls. It is not something which is abstract and aloof - divinity is a part of the very fabric of our being. And because divinity to Wiccans is a reality, not an abstract concept, it is perceived in many forms, but primarily as a Goddess and a God, who have many names and aspects, but always represent the divine force: that Mystery which we cannot know, but seek as best we can to understand.

Wiccans do not "worship" trees or rocks; however, Wiccans do revere the divine life force which is contained within trees and rocks; indeed, is contained within every part of the universe. The Sky Father and Earth Mother are two very conventional God and Goddess forms. However, the Egyptians worshipped a Sky Goddess in Nuit, and an Earth God in Geb. Many cultures revered the solar principle as male, and the lunar current as female; others reversed this, and worshipped a male Moon God, and female Sun Goddess. It is important to remember that Pagan deities express divinity made manifest in many different ways.

Wicca is what is called a "Mystery" religion. That is, a religion which requires its followers to undergo a ceremony in which certain teachings are made known to them, and certain experiences undergone. This is known as "initiation", and all Wiccans are initiated as either a Priest, or a Priestess: there is no Wiccan "congregation". There are no Wiccan prophets, messiahs or saints; each individual makes their own attempt to understand what they can about the "mystery" which we call life.

We are often asked whether self-initiation is possible, and if so, is it considered to be effective? This is a difficult question to answer, for much depends upon the individual, and their circumstances.

"The purpose of the rite of initiation is to effect a spiritual awakening of the initiate and to link him or her to the group mind of Wicca."

(Wicca by Vivianne Crowley: Aquarian Press 1989). Initiation also serves to admit a newcomer to a particular coven and tradition. However: "The Way of Initiation is not a mundane organisation, but is a psychic method of leading to spiritual attainment. No society or fraternity has a monopoly of its teachings, neither has any of them the power to convey the full range of its initiations." (Sane Occultism by Dion Fortune: Aquarian Press 1987).

Initiation rituals can vary greatly in their exoteric form, but generally have a similar esoteric core. Some Wiccans adhere very strictly to the rite used by Gardner; others have made a few changes, and some use a different ritual entirely. All are equally valid, provided that they serve to "effect a spiritual awakening", as Vivianne so beautifully puts it.

The question of self-initiation is one which causes a lot of dissension, although lately, it has become accepted that some Wiccans have no choice but to initiate themselves. "After all, Wicca and all religions serve one major purpose: to facilitate communication with Deity. If self-dedicated Wiccans establish relationships with the Goddess and God, observe Wiccan holidays, use Wiccan tools and uphold Wiccan ideals, what initiate can dare state that they aren't Wiccan?" (The Truth about Witchcraft Today by Scott Cunningham: Llewellyn 1988).

A rather strong viewpoint, but one which finds some sympathy among modern Wiccans. Writing in 1978, Doreen Valiente included a ritual for self-initiation in her book, "Witchcraft for Tomorrow" (pub. Hales). In the introduction she says, "Many people, I know, will question the idea of self-initiation, as given in this book. To them I will address one simple question: who initiated the first witch?"

There is one very simple fact implicit within any initiation: it is not the external form of the ritual that is important, but whether the participants enact the rite with sincerity, and in a manner designed to awaken within the initiate an aware- ness of the Mystery, which leads to contact with the divine force. When this happens, the parochial limitations of a tradition or sect are surpassed by the connection that

4

the initiate makes with the divine. It is this to which Dion Fortune refers when she says that, "No society or fraternity has a monopoly of its teachings...".

However, an experienced initiator can lead the way to the gate of initiation, and although they cannot make the journey on the initiate's behalf, they can certainly show the way, and provide a map. Writing in the magazine Children of Sekhmet (Vol 3 No 4), Julia made the point that, "Self-initiation is the hardest of all, similar to attempting a journey without a map or guide, having first to find your way out of a room which does not appear to have a door...". Not impossible by any means, but certainly a deal more difficult than following a map which has been given to you by one who has made the journey already, and who is able to open the doorway for you.

Both Gardnerian and Alexandrian Wiccan traditions share a common source in the "Mystery Religions", where entry to a group is by way of a formal initiation, performed by the group Elders upon the newcomer, sometimes called a neophyte. After initiation, the neophyte becomes a 1st degree Wiccan (or Witch) and is taught by others in his or her coven the skills of healing, and the ways of making magic. However, whilst this teaching is considered of the utmost importance, Wiccans never lose sight of the fact that Wicca is a RELIGION, and whilst its practices may include the performance of magic and spells, the worship of the God and Goddess are paramount. The techniques which are used may be called occultism, magic, meditation, and so on, but it is important not to make the mistake of confusing the technique with the purpose.

There are no hard and fast rules about when 1st degree initiates may be further initiated to 2nd degree, but it would be rare for this to happen before they had worked for at least a year and a day within their parent coven. All of the Wiccan initiations are extremely powerful experiences, and almost without exception cause major changes within the initiate's psyche and of course, within their life. For this reason, Wiccan initiations are taken very seriously, and are a great responsibility to those who perform them.

Different Wiccan traditions have different attitudes towards the 2nd (and indeed, 3rd) degrees, but in one main essential they agree: 2nd degree Wiccans have authority to initiate and teach others, and are able to gather together a group of their own, should they wish to do so. There is one further degree: the 3rd. In some traditions, this is taken by a 2nd degree couple who formally establish a magical, working partnership for the purpose of running their own coven. Other traditions offer a 3rd degree ritual, which can be taken either by a solitary or a couple, depending upon individual circumstances.

For a more detailed discussion of the Wiccan initiation rites we cannot recommend too highly Vivianne Crowley's excellent book, "Wicca: the Old Religion in the New Age" (Aquarian, 1989).

CHAPTER TWO

WHAT DO I NEED?

The short, sharp answer to this is - nothing! However, there are certain items which have become accepted as Wiccan tools, and others which are commonly used during rituals. None of them are "essential" to the worship of the God and Goddess, but are useful for us poor humans to use as a focus of our intent, and to help us make that contact with divinity which is, after all, the whole point.

Incidentally, Wiccans are adept at making the best use of everyday items, and whilst having an ornate silver chalice might be your dream, a simple pottery cup will suffice just as well. Be guided by your financial status, your aesthetic taste, and your intuition!

THE ALTAR

A small table, box, chest of drawers or other similar article is ideal. We have found a pine "toybox" to be very useful, but the most practical is a chest of drawers, or cupboard with a front opening. This gives you sufficient space to store various items, and if you forget something, you don't have to move everything while you lift up the lid to get it! When working out of doors, a tree stump, a rock, or even the ground, are all suitable to use as an altar. (Although we would add here that a tree stump indoors is also a very nice altar.)

ALTAR CLOTH

If you like to use an altar cloth, make sure that it is always clean. Iron it after washing, and keep it solely for use as an altar cloth.

THE ATHAME

Pronounced "A-thay-me", with a slight emphasis upon the second syllable. This is a dagger which normally has a black or dark wood handle. However, many Wiccans we know have an athame that does not have a black handle, and it is quite acceptable to use anything which appeals to you personally. In most traditions it is not, under any circumstances, used to draw blood, and therefore need not be sharp. However, some traditions have a practice of consecrating their athame with their own blood, and if this appeals to you, then obviously the knife has to be sharp enough to prick your skin. The Wiccan athame is used to direct power in a circle, and should fit comfortably in your hand. If you perform a ritual in a public area, make sure that you only use a dagger if local laws permit it. Some traditions in Britain (not either Gardnerian or Alexandrian) forbid the presence of metal at a ritual; these people use a carved wooden dagger in its stead.

THE WHITE-HANDLED KNIFE

Also a dagger, but as its name implies, with a white hilt. This tool is used to carve, cut, and scrape, and therefore normally has a cutting edge, and may also be sharply pointed. Some people have incorrectly called the white handled knife a boline or burin - these are quite different, being small pointed metal spikes, commonly used to puncture or scratch. They are not daggers. However, they can be useful (for engraving, leatherwork, etc.), and are quite often found within a Wiccan's set of ritual tools.

THE WAND

Normally of wood, and traditionally the length of your arm from elbow to finger point. There are many kinds of Wiccan wand, and include the classic "magician's" wand of black and white; a phallic wand; a plain piece of wood; a staff; a walking stick, and so on. The most important thing is that you should put some effort into creating your own wand, even if it is only polishing or varnishing the finished object.

THE CUP

In fact, most Wiccans have two cups, or chalices. One to hold the water which is blessed to consecrate the working space; the other to hold the wine or fruit juice which is blessed at the end of the ritual. They can be made of just about anything, from simple cups, to elaborate chalices.

THE PENTACLE

This is a flat disk, which again can be made of almost any material, but is commonly copper, brass, or wood. Beeswax is also a very good medium to use to make a pentacle, and has the benefit of being easy to engrave should you wish to include signs or sigils upon its surface. The most common signs are shown below in figure 1. Many Wiccans use the pentacle to hold the salt which is used during the consecration of the working space. As salt is very corrosive, we would recommend that you use a small glass or pottery dish to contain it, and place that, rather than the salt itself, upon your pentacle.

Figure 1

Meaning of the symbols: The upright pentagram crowned with an upright triangle is the symbol of the 3rd degree. The inverted pentagram is the symbol of the 2nd degree (and is not to be confused with any pseudo-Satanic symbols beloved of Hollywood and the media!). The inverted triangle is the symbol of the 1st degree. The circle crowned by a semicircle represents the Horned God; the two adjoining crescents represent the Goddess. The plain S symbolises a kiss, and the S with a stroke symbolises the scourge.

THE CORDS

Cords of certain colours and lengths are used during Wiccan initiations, but for general use, you can have any colour which seems appropriate to you, and choose whatever length you feel will be of most use. As a rough guide, a cord of about three metres in length will probably be sufficient for your needs. You can buy coloured cords from most shops which sell fabrics, or you can refer to Chapter 7, where you will find simple instructions for making your own.

THE CENSER

Incense is commonly used during Wiccan rites. This may be in the form of an incense stick or cone, or loose gums and herbs burnt upon hot charcoal. Whichever form you use will require a container. Hot charcoal should be placed on a bed of sand at least 4 inches deep, which is contained within a pot of some kind. Pottery or metal are ideal; wood should be avoided, as the charcoal reaches very high temperatures. A word of warning: never place a censer on a heat-sensitive surface! If you use incense sticks, then a holder which has been designed to catch the ash as it falls, or a pot of earth or sand in which the stick can be placed, will be fine.

THE SWORD

Some Wiccan covens use a Sword, but its use is optional, and certainly not essential for anyone starting to practise Wicca.

THE SCOURGE

This tool is a symbol of spirit, but its use and purpose is taught only within a coven, and is not essential for those who are working outside of a traditional coven environment. Like most of the tools it can be made from almost anything, but traditionally it has a wooden handle, with eight leather thongs, each containing five knots. Some modern covens have dispensed with using the scourge.

CANDLES AND CANDLESTICKS

Wiccans generally have one or two candles upon their altar, as well as one candle in each of the cardinal points of the working area. If you need to put candles on the floor, or are performing your ritual out of doors, then the glass jar type of candles are ideal (called "patio candles".) You can make your own by using washed-out jam or coffee jars, and setting the candle in them on a layer of melted candle wax. If you are performing your ritual indoors, then any candlestick or candle holder will suffice. A word of warning: make sure that all candles are firm and steady, and well away from anything which might catch alight (e.g., curtains, dried flower arrangements, hems of robes, etc.).

REPRESENTATION OF THE GOD AND GODDESS

As a reminder that ALL Wiccan practices are performed under the guidance of the God and Goddess, and in their honour, Wiccans generally have some symbols to represent the God and Goddess upon their altar. The most common are pictures or statues of deities which are meaningful to you, but just as good are things like shells or stones (to represent the Goddess), and pine cones or seeds (to represent the God). It is your understanding of the deities that should determine the symbol you use to represent them. And remember: it is a symbol only. God and Goddess exist in everything, and in every place. Your symbols are there to serve as a reminder of the powers of divinity, and are not the God and Goddess themselves.

FLOWERS OR PLANTS

In older days, the Festivals were celebrated in accordance with the natural cycle, but since the coming of Christianity, "dates" have replaced "seasons", and modern mankind has generally divorced itself from the natural world. However, Wicca is a religion which seeks to understand the turning of the seasons, and so we are consciously attempting to re-contact that natural world. One of the ways we do this is to place some vegetation upon the altar which expresses the time of year. Not bundles of it, nor flowers from a florist; just something that is growing naturally in your own environment at that time of year to act as a reminder of what is happening in the natural world.

In the northern hemisphere, traditional plants would be Holly (Yule); Snowdrops (Candlemas); Daffodils (Spring Equinox); Hawthorn Blossom (Beltane); Oak Leaves (Summer Solstice); Wheat (Lammas); Acorns and Pine Cones (Autumn Equinox); Elderberries (Samhain). The most important thing is to use the vegetation which expresses the principle of the Festival, and which occurs naturally at that time of year.

For example; on the east coast of England, which is cold and bleak, sometimes the Hawthorn does not bloom until July, which is far too late for Beltane. On the coast of West Wales however, where it is much warmer, the Hawthorn could have bloomed and dropped by Beltane. So, although the tradition is for Hawthorn at Beltane, if it is not available, then something which is in bloom at that time of year is used instead.

In Australia, the blooming of the wattle is at precisely the correct time of year for Candlemas. So, our coven practice since being in NSW has been to have some wattle on the altar for our Candlemas rite. In Canberra, which is colder than Sydney, the wattle is in full bloom by the Spring Equinox. We have a large oak tree near our home, so we use some its leaves for our Midsummer Rite. The tree also produces its acorns at precisely the right time of year for the Autumn Equinox (naturally; trees have never been told the "names" of the months, and so do not have the same problems as humans adjusting to the southern hemisphere cycle!), so we use a sprig of oak leaves with acorns attached for our Autumn Equinox rite. If the oak tree were not here, then we would look around for something which expresses the same principle of a ripened fruit, or a seed waiting to fall.

Wherever you live, you will find - if you look for it - trees and plants that grow, bloom, fade and die, all in accordance with the seasons. All you have to do is become aware of the natural world around you. And once you start to follow the Wiccan way, this will become second nature to you.

ROBES

This is entirely a matter of personal taste. If you are working on your own, and have somewhere private to perform your rituals, then you can choose to be naked (skyclad), or wear robes which have been specially made or bought for ritual use. If you are working with other people, or in a less private environment, then you will probably need to wear clothes of some sort. If you have a simplistic approach to your Wiccan practices, then you may feel comfortable performing your ritual wearing your everyday clothes. However, there are some very good reasons for either working skyclad, or obtaining a robe which you wear for all your rituals. Firstly, it helps you make that change of consciousness from the "everyday" to the "magical" when you remove your normal clothes, and either put on something special, or work naked. Secondly, wearing a robe, or being skyclad, is something that you are unlikely to do during your day-to-day activities, and it re-affirms that you are performing an act which is special to you.

If you are reasonably adequate with a needle, then you could make your own robe without too much trouble. Most pattern books (which can be found in any shop or department which sells fabric) include simple robe patterns; some of the best are in the "fancy dress" section. If you really are absolutely hopeless at sewing, and have no idea where to start, then you will probably be able to find a seamstress to make a robe for you quite easily. Either by asking in the fabric shop or department, or by looking in your local paper in the small ads section. One word of advice: avoid robes which have large sleeves! From a practical point of view, these are a disaster. You will either catch the sleeve in a candle flame, or simply knock something over as you reach across your altar. Also make sure that you are able to move your legs easily, as many Wiccan rituals include dancing in a circle.

You will only wear your robe during your rituals, and should try to keep it apart from your other clothes when not in use. Good fabrics to use are silk, cotton or wool; try to avoid synthetics if possible, and particularly anything which has a tendency to flare up quickly if a flame should catch it.

RITUAL DIARY

This is nothing more than a simple book in which you can record your rituals, and any subsequent events that are of interest. Sample entry:

Full moon ritual 9 August 1991, Moon in Leo. Location: Normal site (outdoors) Those present: (list the names of participants) Work: healing for Roger's leg.

Method: We visualised Roger sitting in his bed at home, and chanted the healing rune and concentrated on mending the broken bone. We channelled blue healing energy, and tried to visualise Roger with a completely healed leg, no limp.

Notes: Three of us "heard" Roger speaking during the ritual, and were sure that we were in astral contact with him. This is to be checked out with Roger later. Also, we saw a wombat in the bush as we were clearing away, and this is an animal with which Roger has a very strong affinity. We think this may be a good omen.

Follow-up: Leave a space here for later entries to be made concerning the success or failure of the ritual, and for any other points of interest. For example, Julia's Coven in London used blue energy in one absent healing ritual, and were encouraged to learn some time later that the person being healed started to wear blue clothes; a colour she did not usually wear. In Australia, our coven performed absent healing for someone, using a pink quartz crystal as a focus. We discovered that the day after the ritual, the person wore pink - again, a colour she would not normally wear. These are indications that a magical link has been effectively made.

CONSECRATION OF WORKING TOOLS

It is customary for working tools employed during Wiccan rituals to be purified and consecrated before they are used. This is rather a chicken and egg situation, as most books will tell you that they can only be consecrated in a space which has been erected using consecrated tools! However, there is a way round the problem, which we explain in chapter 4, so will say no more about that here.

CHAPTER THREE

SETTING UP

OUTDOORS

Find a place where you will not be disturbed, and sweep or clear sticks, stones, and other debris from the area where you intend to work. This is very important! We know of one quite large ritual held out of doors in Australia, where the organisers did not first clear the working site. The participants, who had been asked to remove their shoes, suffered many cuts and bruises as a result. So, spend a short time sweeping and clearing the site.

It is likely that you will have taken a shower or bath before leaving home, but if you are holding your ritual near to natural water (e.g., sea or river), then you could swim after you have set up your tools, instead of taking a shower or bath.

INDOORS

Sweep or vacuum the area where you intend to work. Disconnect the telephone, and if you have any pets, make sure that they are somewhere safe. If you share your home with others, make sure they all know you are not to be disturbed. Have a shower or bath after you have finished setting up, and put on your robe if you intend wearing one.

BOTH

Make sure that all the tools and equipment you intend to use are clean, and you have everything you need.

Your altar can be placed in the centre, in the east, or in the "dark" quarter, which in the northern hemisphere is north, and in the southern hemisphere, south.

Before we explain the reasons for this, we need to look briefly at the solar cycle, as it is this which traditionally determines much of Wiccan (and magical) practice. Wherever you are on the earth, the Sun appears to rise in the east, and will set in the west. This does not change. What does differ from northern to southern hemisphere though is the actual passage of the Sun in the heavens. Because of the tilt of the Earth as it spins on its axis (which gives us our seasons), the Sun appears to move towards the equator; thus in the northern hemisphere the Sun appears to move via the south, but in the southern hemisphere the Sun appears to move via the northern quarter. The further north or south of the equator the more apparent the arc, and the more noticeable the effect. Matthew observed this particularly after working in far north Queensland where the Sun appeared to move almost directly overhead. He then flew to southern Tasmania, where it was obvious that the Sun was far lower in the sky and moved in a lower arc across the northern horizon. However, although the degree of the arc changed, the direction of the actual movement of the Sun was still noticeable.

We will return to this subject later, when we discuss the Wiccan Wheel of the Year, but at the moment, back to the altar! As we said above, the altar is commonly placed either in the east, the centre, or in the "dark" quarter.

EAST is the place of the rising Sun, and many magical systems locate their altar in this quarter. The reasons for this are that in magical philosophy, all things begin in the east, the place of the rising Sun. Therefore in magical practice (which seeks to replicate the heavens on earth), all things are begun in the east.

NORTH or SOUTH is the "dark quarter" depending upon whether you are in the northern or southern hemisphere, as we explained above. Many books which describe Wiccan practice will simply tell the reader that the altar is placed in the north. This is because those books are written by practitioners who live in the northern hemisphere, where the north is the one place where the Sun never shines, and is therefore the place of mystery. In many northern mythologies, it is the place where the gods "live". There are a number of reasons for this, but a primary one relates to the fact that mankind cannot perceive what happens in the "dark quarter", and so by allocating this place to the gods, we express that we acknowledge the "mystery", without being able directly to perceive it. So, the Wiccan practice of placing the altar in the "dark quarter" is directly related to our desire to link the focal point of our circle with our gods.

CENTRE is a common practice if the meeting place, and numbers of people attending, allow a centrally placed altar. Generally speaking, with an altar in the centre, when you stand before it you will face either east, north or south, in accordance with the principles explained above. Some groups orient the altar in accordance with the seasonal cycle: if you wish to do this in the southern hemisphere, then the altar at the Spring Equinox would face east, the place of beginnings and the rising Sun. At the Summer Solstice it would face north, the place where the Sun is at its height. At the Autumn Equinox it would face west, the place where the Sun sets, and at the Winter Solstice, it would face south, for this is the longest night of the year, and thus the "darkest night". Therefore the altar at Candlemas would face south east; at Beltane, north east; at Lammas, north west, and at Samhain, south west. In the northern hemisphere, the altar at the Spring Equinox would still face east, the place of beginnings and the rising Sun. At the Summer Solstice though it would face south, the place where the Sun is at its height. At the Autumn Equinox it would again face west, the place where the Sun sets, and at the Winter Solstice, it would face north, for in the northern hemisphere the longest night of the year, and thus the "darkest night", is when the sun is in the north. The altar at Candlemas would face north east; at Beltane, south east; at Lammas, south west, and at Samhain, north west. Place upon your altar all those tools which you need for your ritual, set out in a way which is pleasing to you, and allows you to reach everything easily, without knocking things over. Place your four quarter candles in their correct positions: there are a number of colours that can be used, including, of course, simple white. Another common standard arrangement is a yellow candle to symbolise the element of AIR; a red candle to symbolise the element of FIRE; a blue candle to symbolise the element of WATER; and a green, brown or black candle to symbolise the element of EARTH. These attributions are commonly used in Wiccan ritual, but derive from The Hermetic Order of the Golden Dawn. Another frequently used set of colours are: blue for AIR, red for FIRE, sea green for WATER and yellow/brown for EARTH.

The position of the elements to the cardinal points is usually as follows: AIR in the east; FIRE in the north (southern hemisphere) or south (northern hemisphere); WATER in the west; EARTH in the south (southern hemisphere) or north (northern hemisphere).

It is important to remember that these candles are merely a symbolic representation of the four elements, not the elements themselves. The arrangement of element to cardinal direction may appear to be intellectually arbitrary; however, continued use with this arrangement (and when we were in Britain, with its northern hemisphere equivalent) has proven quite conclusively that there is a very real and objective reality to these positions. However, your own intuition and experience should be the primary guide when determining the colour and location of your elemental symbols.

A number of Wiccans have changed the orientation of the elements to suit the closest geographical representation of each element. For example, in Sydney, on the east coast of Australia, with a great landmass to the west, it is not unusual to find the water candle in the east, and the earth candle in the west. With this arrangement, the fire candle usually appears in the north, with air in the south. However, it is not so important which system you use, but that you understand WHY you are using it.

NB: if you are working out of doors in a fire risk area, and/or during a fire risk period, do not, under any circumstances, use a naked flame of any kind. Even on a beach, sparks can carry to nearby bushland, and cause untold damage to bushland and homes. No matter how safely you think you have set your candles, accidents can happen.

For summer rituals in a hot climate, consider working during daylight hours, when candles are unnecessary. With a little imagination, you will be able to think of numerous other symbols to represent the elements.

Finally, here is a final checklist of things which most altars contain, and most rituals use:

Athame
Cup containing clean water
Pentacle, and dish containing salt
Censer and either incense stick, or charcoal and loose incense
Candle(s) for the altar
God and Goddess symbols
Flowers, plant or other vegetation
Cup containing wine or fruit juice and plate of cake or biscuits
Quarter candles
Matches or lighter and a taper
Ritual diary and a couple of pens

Any additional items which you need for your ritual, or would like to have on your altar

Most rituals conclude with either a simple meal, or elaborate feast, depending upon the occasion and the participants. This is up to each individual, but it is a good idea to make sure you eat and drink something after ritual work. It is an excellent way to "ground", particularly if you have to drive home.

CHAPTER FOUR

ERECTING YOUR WORKING SPACE

Wiccans normally perform their rituals in a "circle". Why? You might well ask! The reasons are many and varied, but we will deal with as many of them as are relevant in a book of this kind.

1)   If you travel throughout northern Europe, Wicca's homeland, you will encounter many hundreds of neolithic structures called "stone circles". In Australia, concentric circles (rather similar to the European neolithic ring and cup marks) form an import part of Aboriginal art, and feature in many Dreamtime stories. We will talk about the energy that exists in these circles a little later, but for now, it is important to appreciate that the circle is a very potent and powerful focus of Earth energy.

2)   If you look up to the heavens, you will see our two most important symbols - the Sun and Moon - in their circular form. Further, when you observe the "movement" of any these, or any planet or star in the sky, it is clear that the motion is a circular one.

3)   If you stand on a flat plain (in Australia, this is not difficult once you leave the cities!) you seem to be standing in the middle of a vast circle. Thus our vision describes a circular horizon when conditions allow.

4)   And finally, Wicca is a religion of equals: although individual covens have their leaders, and there are degrees of expertise, no-one "rules" another, and all have equal status when gathered in a circle.

Whether you are working indoors or outside, you will normally begin all your rituals by defining the area which is your working space. This

DOES NOT have to be a physical circle, marked on the floor! In the art of magic, the most powerful tool you have is your mind. When you define with a ritual act the area in which you are going to work, you visualise the circle which surrounds you; you do not need to draw it out. Most Wiccans visualise a sphere rather than a two- dimensional circle, but this is something which you will have to determine for yourself.

We would now like to explain something about the way in which a circle is erected (or cast, is the more common term), which takes us back to the stone circles of Europe. If you stand inside a stone circle, you are more than likely going to feel a very definite "tug" of energy moving in a circular direction. This direction will normally be clockwise. (We say "more than likely" and "normally" because some circles seem to have been constructed for very specific purposes and do not accord with these general principles.) There are three main reasons for this:

1)   We may not know why stone circles were constructed, but we do know that they were built in accordance with the rising and setting of heavenly bodies; often the Sun. Stonehenge is perhaps the best known, but there are many others. The circular pattern of the circles replicates on Earth the motions of the heavens: As Above, So Below, in the well-known Hermetic axiom.

2)   There is a geophysical force which is known as the CORIOLIS EFFECT. This was discovered by a French civil engineer in the 19th century, and explains the deflection in the path of a body moving relative to the Earth, when viewed from the Earth. It is due to the Earth's rotation - in the northern hemisphere the deflection is clockwise; in the southern hemisphere, it is anti-clockwise. The Coriolis effect was (and is) of vital importance to sailing, for it is what determines the direction of cyclone activity, and was used to map the effects of the world's winds.

3)   Stone circles in Europe seem to have been sited at points where

a conjunction of Earth energies takes place. Similarly, at least some Aboriginal sacred sites in Australia occur where the Earth energy has a potent circular force. Thus the Earth currents (which can be felt by those attuned to them wherever they may be), are focused by means of a circle. Similarly the mazes (which are also found all over Europe) are constructed in circular form, and like the stone circles, are concentrations of Earth energy.

So, we can summarise the Wiccan circle as being both a focus of Earth energy, and a symbolic representation on Earth of the motion of the heavens. Like all magic - a combination of the heavens and the Earth: As Above, So Below. For when we cast, or visualise, a circle, we are attempting to create a microcosm - a "little world" - which contains all that is found in the macrocosm - the "great world". Therefore we ensure that we follow the energies of our physical location; we also ensure that we follow - as our ancestors did when they constructed the stone circles - the motions of the heavens.

There is a very strong tradition which is consistent throughout all magical systems, that except for certain types of banishing, or rituals which utilise a "chaotic" energy, all movements to cast and consecrate the circle, and all movements subsequently made within the circle, are made in a DEOSIL direction. Similarly, magic of increase is performed when the Moon is waxing, and magic of decrease when the Moon is waning.

It is worth spending a little time here defining DEOSIL and WIDDERSHINS, for there is a great deal of confusion about what these terms actually mean. DEOSIL (deasil or deiseal) refers to any movement made in a direction which is in accordance with, "the apparent course of the sun (a practice held auspicious by the Celts)." [Oxford English Dictionary: 1991, 2nd edition]

The OED gives several examples of the use of the word Deosil:

"1771: At marriages and baptisms they make a processions round the church, Deasoil, i.e., sunways."

"1814: The surgeon.. perambulated his couch three times, moving from east to west, according to the course of the sun.. which was called making the deasil."

"1875: There was a sacred stone in Jura round which the people used to move `deasil', i.e., sunwise."

Although the word 'deosil' is associated with concepts of the right hand, and of motion which is "with continuous turning to the right", you must remember that these concepts are directly derived from the apparent motion of the Sun. In Europe, where this word originated, that motion is east, south, west and north; i.e., clockwise. If sundials had been invented in Australia instead of Europe, clockwise would be the other way!

Wiccans in the southern hemisphere must keep this in mind whenever they read any books about magic or Wicca that have been written by authors in the northern hemisphere. Some of them may say to "reverse" the directions when working in the southern hemisphere, but many northern hemisphere writers are themselves completely unaware of the differences between the two hemispheres. Also, if the book is an ancient one, it would simply not have occurred to the author that one day, his readers would include those who live in lands which had not yet been "discovered"!

WITHERSHINS (widdershins) has two main definitions in the OED:

   1) In a direction opposite to the usual; the wrong way...

   2)   In a direction contrary to the apparent course of the Sun (considered as unlucky or causing disaster).

Associated words - all with malefic inference - are: witherward (hostile, inimical); witherwin (and enemy, adversary); withersake (also an enemy or an adversary).

Wiccan philosophy does not subscribe to the viewpoint that widdershins is either "evil" or "unlucky", but it is most definitely seen as a contrary motion. Certain types of banishing, or rituals to mark the decrease of something, could justifiably use a widdershins motion. We give one example in chapter 5 of widdershins working in a healing ritual used in our coven; there are many other uses, but these are all, without exception, specific workings against the motion of the Sun. In normal circle workings, all movements are made deosil, i.e. "with the sun".

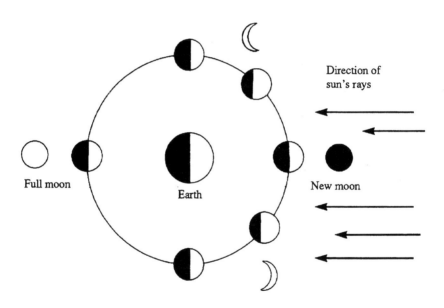

Fig 2: The Phases of the Moon

Of course we know that in fact the Sun does not move at all, and it is the Earth revolving upon its axis which makes the Sun, planets and stars appear to move in the heavens. It is also this rotation of the Earth upon its axis which enables us to see the Moon every day, except during its "dark" phase, when it is "outshone" by the Sun. The Moon orbits the Earth once every (approximately) twenty-eight days. When it is between the Earth and the Sun, it is "New", and cannot be seen from the Earth. As it moves away from a position between the Earth and Sun, it can be seen first as a sliver, then growing through its crescent phase to Full Moon, when it is actually on the far side of the Earth from the Sun. Remember that what we see of the Moon is actually the reflection of the Sun's rays from its surface. After it is Full, the Moon travels back around the Earth, gradually diminishing in size until once more it is New, and positioned between the Earth and the Sun.

Perhaps this is also a good place to mention the differences in the appearance of the Moon between southern and northern hemispheres. Most books will tell you that the waxing Moon looks like figure 2a, and the waning Moon like figure 2b. So it does - in the northern hemisphere! In the southern hemisphere, the horns of the Moon point in the other direction, as shown in figures 3a (waxing Moon) and 3b (waning Moon). In both hemispheres you will occasionally see the Moon's horns pointing upwards, as shown in figure 3c, and also at various degrees of inclination between horizontal and vertical.

Fig 2a.   Fig 2b.

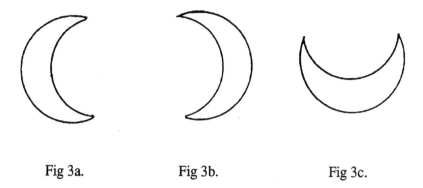

Fig 3a.   Fig 3b.   Fig 3c.

Casting the circle

You have your altar set up with all the necessary items (refer to the check-list in the previous chapter), and if outdoors, the site has been cleared and swept. You are either skyclad or robed, or if you prefer, are wearing everyday clothes, and are now ready to begin. Light the altar and quarter candles, and the incense stick, or charcoal, and place in the censer. If you are using loose incense, have some ready to place on the charcoal. NB: if you are using charcoal disks, do not light them near an altar cloth, or anything else which can be damaged if a spark flies off and lands on it - including yourself, especially if working skyclad! Needless to say, outdoor rituals during fire danger periods should NOT utilise any naked flame. Even a stray spark from a charcoal disk could begin a bush fire.

The following method is one example of how to create a sacred working space. Each tradition has its own circle casting ritual, and even within a single tradition, individual groups have their own variations. The following is intended to provide a simple guide, not a set of definitive instructions! If this one does not appeal to you, choose another from from one of the many published rituals, or of course, you

27

can always write your own. If you join an existing coven, you will be taught the method which is used by that particular group. Whichever ritual you use, just remember that the aim is to construct a sacred space.

Enter your working area, and kneel or stand in front of your altar for a few moments, and allow your mind to focus upon your purpose. Now make an effort to "contact" the God and Goddess, and ask for their blessing upon you, and upon any work which you intend to perform. If you are working in a group, each person performs this silent meditation in turn, and then stands towards the perimeter of the working area. The person casting the circle is the last to make their private meditation at the altar.

The circle has now to be cast: there are a number of different ways of doing this, and all are equally valid. The one we describe here is essentially the Alexandrian form, which has been published in varying amounts of detail in a number of books (See Appendix A for recommended book list), and is quite widely known.

Take the athame, and hold it firmly at arm's length, pointing straight ahead of you, but slightly raised. (If you do not use an athame, wherever it is mentioned from now on, point instead, or use a wand if you prefer.) Start to move around the circle, holding the athame firmly but without being tense, and visualise a circle or sphere forming as you pass around. Some traditions begin casting from the east, others from the dark quarter. It is a matter for you to decide, whatever seems most appropriate. For the sake of simplicity, we would suggest that you start casting your circle from the point you face when standing in front of your altar. Continue describing the circle until you have completed at least one pass through three hundred and sixty degrees. If you go round more than once, that is fine, but you MUST go round at least one complete circuit.

As you cast the circle you can say some words which state what it is you are trying to do. There are many versions of words that can be spoken, or you can remain silent. Avoid at all costs carrying round a crib sheet to read whilst attempting to concentrate on casting a circle! The brain engages a different set of faculties for reading than it uses for the altered state of consciousness which is required for magical work. Basically, if you are reading something, then your mind is operating in a left-brain "analytical" mode which makes it difficult to focus upon "magical" tasks. This is one of the reasons that most Wiccan "chants" and "runes" are very simple rhyming verses. They cause the left-brain activities to be put out of the way, and allow the right-brain to function in its magical (intuitive) mode.

The left-hand hemisphere of the brain is generally the most dominant, and its functions of reasoning, time-telling and analytical thought processes have been developed from early childhood. The right-hand hemisphere is the spatially aware and conceptual part of the brain. It is used predominantly in art, music, daydreaming, magic, and religious experiences. By giving the left-hand hemisphere something that it cannot do well, or finds boring, (e.g., chanting, runes, etc.), we allow the right-hand hemisphere to take precedence. Thus the left-hand hemisphere remains subdued, and is content to allow the right-hand hemisphere to be dominant during that period.

Therefore, if you read something, you are simply encouraging the left-hand hemisphere to surface once again, imposing its analytical functions upon the intuitive mode of the right-hand hemisphere.

Of course there is no need to say anything out loud as you cast a circle if you would prefer not to, as it is your frame of mind, and the visualisation, which are important, not any lines which you speak. However, most people do like to say something, and we give below a suggestion of some suitable words that can be used. We have not specified any particular God or Goddess names, as it is important that you use ones with whom you personally identify, or who are associated with the particular type of season or magic for which your ritual is being performed. Some Wiccans do not name their deities, and refer to them simply as "Lord and Lady", or "God and Goddess". If you do wish to use deity names, avoid mixing different pantheons; e.g., Apollo (Greek) and Freya (Norse). Not only are they from different cultures, but they haven't been formally introduced, and their respective partners would not be too impressed!

Example of words for the circle casting:

"I conjure thee O circle of power, that thou be a boundary between this world and the realms of the Mighty Ones; a place of peace and joy where we may meet in love and trust for the worship of the Old Ones; and I bless thee in the names of (Goddess) and (God)."

Make sure that when you finish casting the circle, you are either facing the altar once more, or that you continue moving in a deosil direction until you come back to it.

You now need to consecrate the working area with the four elements. There are many ways to do this; some elaborate, some very simple. Many Wiccans use signs called banishing and invoking pentagrams to first exorcise, and then bless, the elements. That is the method that we will describe here, and have included diagrams to show the ways of casting invoking and banishing elemental pentagrams in Appendix B. We are using the following attributions:

Cup of Water to the Water Element
Dish of Salt to the Earth Element
Censer of Incense to the Air Element
Candle to the Fire Element

(Please remember that we are dealing with a symbolic representation of the elements: these are not the magical elements themselves!)

Take the cup of water, and imagine a steady flow of energy coming from the ground beneath you, and the heavens above you. Imagine this flow of energy as a column of light, which mingles with the energy of your own body.

Now imagine this energy passing along your arm, to your hand, and through your athame. Perform the banishing Earth pentagram over the top of the cup saying: "I cast out from thee all ills and impurities of the spirit". Now perform the invoking Water pentagram saying: "And I do bless thee and consecrate thee in the names of (Goddess) and (God)."

Take the dish of salt, and again, imagine a steady flow of energy coming from the ground beneath you, the heavens above you, and your own body, passing down through your athame. The salt is not exorcised, for being pure in itself, it is not seen as necessary, so you simply perform the invoking Earth pentagram over the salt saying: "I bless thee and consecrate thee in the names of (Goddess) and (God)." Now tip the salt into the water, and stir it with your athame. Carry the cup around the perimeter of the circle (normally the boundary of your working area), sprinkling the water/salt as you go. Move in a deosil direction, sprinkling water upon anyone who is in the circle, as well as upon the ground. Complete at least one full pass around the circle, and then replace the cup upon the altar.

Now take the incense stick, or place some incense upon the hot charcoal. Imagine the flow of energy passing through your athame once more, and then perform the banishing Earth pentagram over the top of the censer saying: "I cast out from thee all ills and impurities of the spirit", then perform the invoking Air pentagram saying: "And I do bless thee and consecrate thee in the names of (Goddess) and (God)." Take the censer and walk once again around the perimeter of the circle moving in a deosil direction, and allowing the incense smoke to perfume the area and anyone in the circle.

Finally, once more visualising the flow of energy passing through your athame, stand in front of one of the candles upon your altar, and perform the banishing Earth pentagram before the candle flame (or over the top of it) saying: "I cast out from thee all ills and impurities of the spirit", then perform the invoking Fire pentagram saying: "And I do bless thee and consecrate thee in the names of (Goddess) and (God)." Carry the candle around the perimeter of the circle, and then replace it upon the altar. (NB: some Wiccans do not exorcise the flame, believing fire to be a gift from the gods, and therefore sacred and pure already. It is up to you which form you follow.)

If you prefer not to use banishing and invoking pentagrams, it is quite acceptable simply to point at, or insert your athame tip, into each element. Not all Wiccan traditions use pentagrams, and it is up to each individual to decide upon their own preferred style.

As you carry each of the elements around the circle, you are infusing it with the powers of the four elements, and making sure that you have a balanced, and consecrated, space in which to work and offer worship to the God and Goddess. Salt water is a purifying agent; salt has always been used to preserve and purify, and water to cleanse.

As you carry the salt water around your circle, and sprinkle it upon all those who are present, you are carrying out an age-old act of purification and consecration. Keep this in mind as you carry the salt water around, for in magic, your intention is all important.

Incense has been used since earliest times as a perfume, and as a "sacrifice" to the gods. By carrying around a censer of sweet smelling incense you are reinforcing the purification and consecration of the circle with the salt water, and also beginning the process of reaching out towards the God and Goddess.

As you carry around your candle flame, you can think about the ways in which fire purifies. Fire is traditionally believed to be the most "divine" of the elements, and so you are continuing that process which connects you with the God and Goddess. You can also think about the balance of the four elements, which have now all contributed to the purification and consecration of your working space.

At this point you formally call upon the powers of the four elements to be present in the circle, which is often called either "erecting the watchtowers" or "invoking the quarters". This takes many forms, from visualising the qualities of the seasons in each quarter (East - Spring; North - Summer; West - Autumn; South - Winter), or actually calling upon a specific Guardian, who is related to that element.

The Guardians that Wiccans use are many and varied. In the northern hemisphere, it is common to find people using the four Greek winds - Boreas, Zephyrus, Notus and Eurus. We have worked with American covens who use "teacher" figures such as Merlin, Prometheus, and so on, and many groups (generally those more attuned to ceremonial magic) quite often use the four archangels. Whatever you choose to use should be a "set": that is, don't use Boreas and Zephyrus coupled with Merlin and Prometheus! If you want to use the winds that's fine, but use ALL of them, not just one or two. You can use male, or female, or androgynous figures - it really is up to you to discover those Guardians with whom you feel most comfortable, and with whom you can easily work. One word of advice though; it is generally considered inappropriate to use Gods and Goddesses as Guardians in the quarters.

So how do you "call upon" the powers of the elements? Simply, by facing the four different directions in turn (called the four quarters), and politely asking if each Guardian will be present, and attend your rites. As with the casting and consecration of the circle, there are many ways to do this, and various forms of words which may be spoken if desired. Many Wiccans use a pentagram at this point to call upon the powers of each element. The technique is to trace the relevant elemental pentagram before you in the air (some Wiccans use only invoking Earth in all four quarters, or simply point), whilst calling - either out loud, or in your mind - to the Guardian of that particular quarter.

The following is a variation upon the classic Alexandrian invocations to the quarter Guardians, oriented to the southern hemisphere; northern hemisphere orientation is shown in parentheses.

"Ye Lords of the Watchtowers of the East, ye Lords of Air; I do ask thee to be present, to witness our rites and guard our circle";

"Ye Lords of the Watchtowers of the North (South), ye Lords of Fire; I do ask thee to be present, to witness our rites and guard our circle";

"Ye Lords of the Watchtowers of the West, ye Lords of Water; I do ask thee to be present, to witness our rites and guard our circle";

"Ye Lords of the Watchtowers of the South (North), ye Lords of Earth; I do ask thee to be present, to witness our rites and guard our circle".

The patriarchal emphasis here has proven a stumbling block to a number of modern Wiccans, and there are many alternatives available which are either feminine, or non-gendered. Incidentally, the word "Watchtower" is derived from a system of Renaissance magic called "Enochian", passed to Wicca via the Hermetic Order of the Golden Dawn. However, the concept of "Watchtower" in the Enochian system of magic is very different indeed to its use within modern Wicca. Some traditions include a phrase in the dark quarter, which is designed to "open the gateway" for the God and Goddess to enter the circle. In our tradition, we do this at the centre (see below), but if you prefer, you could use something like the following for the the dark quarter instead:

"Ye Lords of the Watchtowers of the South (North), ye Lords of Earth; I do ask thee to be present, to witness our rites and guard our circle, and make the gateway wherein may enter our Goddess and God."

Whatever words and/or visualisations you choose to use, the method for calling upon each Guardian is the same: starting in the east, stand facing the perimeter of the circle, and concentrate upon the image of the Guardian, and the element, that you are attempting to contact. If there is a group of you, all face the same direction, and try to make sure that you are all concentrating upon the same image. If you are tracing the pentagrams in the air, make full arm movements, and keep your focus upon the visualisation of the Guardian. When you have finished in the east, move to the north (south in the northern hemisphere), and repeat what you have just done, but for Fire. Then move to the west, where the Water Guardian is called, and finally the south (north in the northern hemisphere), where you call upon the Guardian of Earth. If you make the gateway at this point, as you say the words, "and make the gateway", you should describe an archway before you in the air. In the southern hemisphere, you would touch your athame to the ground by your right foot, and move your arm in a large arc, ending by touching the ground by your left foot. In the northern hemisphere, you would start by your left foot, and end by your right foot.

If you used your athame during the calling of the quarter Guardians, now return it to the altar, or into its scabbard if you wear one.

In our tradition, we now open the gateway for the God and Goddess to enter, and call upon them to be present in the circle. If you are working alone, face the altar, and raise your arms above your head. If there are a group of you, all hold hands and form a circle at the centre, facing inwards (i.e., with your backs to the perimeter of the circle), and raise your arms above your head. This is the moment where, having purified and consecrated your working space, and called upon the Guardians of the Elements, you open the gateway for the God and Goddess, and ask for their presence in the circle. This can be a silent meditation, or something like:

"(Goddess) and (God): we build this circle, a place sacred and apart, in your honour. We now open the gateway between the worlds, and ask you to be present here with us, and fill our circle and our hearts with your love and joy."

After you finish the words (or the silent meditation), slowly lower your arms. This concludes the casting of the circle, and you can now perform any acts of worship and magic. We will talk about those in the next two chapters, so will leap ahead here, and explain how you close the circle.

When you have finished your ritual, the final act before you start to close the circle is the ceremony of cakes and wine (or "bikkies and booze", as one Australian Wiccan described it!) In fact, as long as there is something to eat, and something to drink, it really doesn't matter what you have. Some covens insist that wine (often red) is used in the chalice, others prefer mead. When we were holding a lot of public rituals, we used fruit juice in the chalice, and still quite often do so in our own covens. The "cake" can be anything from home-made moon-shaped biscuits, ordinary shop-bought biscuits, cake, fruit, or just plain bread. Like the contents of the chalice, it is a matter of personal preference - there are no hard and fast rules.

The ceremony of cakes and wine is, by tradition, performed by the officiating Priest and Priestess. However, with many Wiccans today finding that other styles suit their own circumstances or preferences better, many other variations have been written, and are practised regularly by groups and individuals wherever Wicca is found. The example here is a traditional one, but can be adapted to suite individual circumstances:

The Priestess takes her athame, and the Priest holds the chalice or cup. She slowly plunges her athame into the wine (or whatever) as the Priest says: "As the athame is to the male, so the chalice is to the female, and when they are conjoined, they become one in truth and bring forth a great blessing." The Priestess removes her athame from the chalice. She and the Priest exchange a kiss, and then she drinks from the chalice. They kiss again, and he takes a drink.

The chalice is now passed in turn to everyone else in the group. It is important to leave some wine in the chalice as a libation to the God and Goddess. When the chalice has been to everyone present, it is replaced upon the altar.

The Priest now holds the plate of cakes before the Priestess, who touches each cake/biscuit with the tip of her athame as he says: "Queen most secret: bless this food into our bodies bestowing health, wealth, strength and happiness, and that deep joy which is the knowledge of thee." They kiss, and she takes a cake. They kiss again, and he takes a cake, and then passes the plate to everyone else in the circle. Again, at least one cake must be left on the plate as a libation to the God and Goddess. As with all other movements in the circle, the passing of the chalice and plate of cakes is made in a deosil motion - i.e., anti-clockwise in the southern hemisphere, clockwise in the northern hemisphere.

If you are working your ritual alone, the chalice and plate of cakes stay on the altar, but the athame is still used in the same way as above, and the same words can be spoken. Drink some of the wine, and eat some of the cake as described above, and remember to leave some as a libation to the God and Goddess.

A few words at this point about the ceremony of cakes and wine. It is of course the communion between those present in the circle and the God and Goddess, but it is also much more than that. This is the symbolic representation of the union of the God and Goddess which is the essence of creation. The athame and chalice are symbols of the essential polarity from which all life proceeds. The wine in the chalice and the food upon the plate is blessed, and becomes all that was, is, and will be. By drinking the wine, and eating the food you partake of both the mystery of creation, and of its fruits.

So, when the athame is placed into the chalice think about the union of the God and Goddess; of the creation of the universe and of the Earth; and most importantly, think about your own place in the universe as a spiritually divine soul, who is one with the God and Goddess. Remember, we are not celebrating human union here, but divine union.

After cakes and wine, food may be brought into circle for the feast or the circle closed, and food eaten elsewhere. It is usual for the feast to be eaten in circle, but this will be determined by your situation and personal preference. If, for example, some participants have long journeys home, you could close the circle, and then bring the food for the feast into the place where the circle was held. In that way, you can have your feast within the sacred space, but people can leave when they have to, without interrupting the feast for the circle to be formally closed.

To close the circle you should first thank the God and Goddess for their presence, and for their blessings upon you and your work. Then stand in the east, facing the perimeter of your circle, and thank the Guardian of Air for attending your rites, and bid him/her farewell.

Turn to each quarter in turn, in the order east, north, west, south (southern hemisphere) or east, south, west, north (northern hemisphere). As we gave a form of the traditional Alexandrian quarter invocations above, here is a variation from that tradition of those which are commonly used at the end of the rite:

"Ye Lords of the Watchtowers of the East: ye Lords of Air: we thank thee for attending our rites, and do bid thee hail and farewell";

"Ye Lords of the Watchtowers of the North (South); ye Lords of Fire; we thank thee for attending our rites, and do bid thee hail and farewell";

"Ye Lords of the Watchtowers of the West; ye Lords of Water; we thank thee for attending our rites, and do bid thee hail and farewell";

"Ye Lords of the Watchtowers of the South (North); ye Lords of Earth; we thank thee for attending our rites, and do bid thee hail and farewell".

If you used the signs of invoking pentagrams to call upon your Guardians, then you would use banishing pentagrams as you bid them farewell. If you simply pointed at each quarter with your athame to call upon them, then do the same again now. Always remember that if you use invoking pentagrams to call, then you should use banishing pentagrams to release. There is an important magical tenet to keep in mind: however much energy you use to call upon something, you should use at least equal energy to disperse it.

Having thanked, and bidden farewell, to all those who were asked to attend your rites, you now need to make a gateway in the circle so that you (and anyone else) can leave. The easiest way of doing this is to stand at the perimeter of the circle, facing the doorway out of the room, or (if out of doors) the direction that you have designated the entrance and exit. The person who cast the circle generally makes the gateway to leave, but this is not essential. Whoever is doing it should place their palms together with their arms extended before them. Visualise the hands making an opening in the circle, and then separate the arms as though parting a pair of curtains. This is commonly known as "parting the veil", and is often used in magical practice. Once the circle has been "breached" as it were, the energy contained within it will continue to do its work, and will gradually dissipate over a period of days.

There is no danger to anyone in "leaving" the circle in this way. If out of doors, any casual visitors to the site will probably be aware of no more than a sense of focused energy. Mind you, if the casual visitor happens to be a wombat, then it is likely that they will treat your circle with disdain, and place their own inimitable offering upon any slight mound within the sacred space! Every Wiccan that we know in Australia reports the same phenomenon where wombats are concerned: whilst all the other animals will walk around the circle, wombats stomp right across its middle, and in their own charming style, deposit some Earth incense (otherwise known as wombat droppings!) upon anything which takes their fancy!

Before leaving the circle, make sure that all the candles have been extinguished, and that the censer (or incense stick) is safely packed away so that it will not tip over, and is well away from anything which might get burned. Needless to say if you are working out of doors, carefully pack away all your equipment, and make sure that you don't leave any rubbish lying around.

Before we leave this chapter, a word about working tools. We have made reference a number of times to using the various tools that were described in chapter 2. As we said in that chapter, it is traditional for all tools used in a circle to be consecrated; but this poses something of a problem to those working on their own, for you can only properly consecrate your tools in a circle - which has been cast using consecrated tools!

Assuming that you do not know anyone who has a set of consecrated tools, and so would be able to cast a circle for you in which to consecrate your own, we would suggest the following. Cast the circle as described above, using only your hand to direct the energy, and consecrate the elements. If you are working indoors, have a small pot of earth by your altar. When you arrive at the point where we said, "the circle is now cast", consecrate each of your tools as follows:

Athame: sprinkle it with the salt water, pass it through the incense smoke, and then quickly through the candle flame. Then, if you are working out of doors, plunge your athame into the earth; if indoors, stick the blade into the pot of earth. As you do these things, visualise the purifying and consecrating energies of each of the elements being infused into your athame, and finally, as you plunge the knife into the earth, ask for the blessings and guidance of the God and Goddess upon your knife.

Now you must re-cast the circle, using your consecrated athame. There is no need to re-do the whole thing; simply start from your altar, and describe the circle with your athame. Even if you are not going to do anything else in the circle, it is important that you use your athame after its consecration. Now proceed to consecrate your other tools if you wish.

White-handled knife: same as for the athame, but after you remove the knife from the earth, use it to cut or inscribe, rather than re-casting the circle. Typical uses are to inscribe a pentagram upon a candle, which is then lit from the altar candle, or to cut an apple in two, and then bind the two halves together with some thread, after placing some herbs between the halves as an offering to the God and Goddess. You would normally bury the apple somewhere in the bush, your garden, or a local park, after the ritual.

Wand: same as for athame, but take care with the candle; make a very quick pass through the flame, otherwise you will have a scorched wand! Instead of plunging the wand into the earth (as you did for your athame), just touch it to the ground as you ask for the blessings of the God and Goddess upon it. Now take the wand to each quarter in turn, and hold it up in salutation.

Pentacle: same as for athame, but taking care with the candle flame if your pentacle is made of any combustible material, or of anything which would be burned by the flame. After the fire consecration, instead of plunging the pentacle into the earth, sprinkle some of the earth upon its surface. A nice way to use your pentacle after consecrating it is then to sprinkle that earth upon your garden, or in the bush, to help things grow.

Cup or Chalice: one cup will already have consecrated salt water in it, so the best thing to do is to place the tip of your athame into the water, and visualise energy pouring into it from all of the elements. See this consecrating the chalice itself, and then pour some water onto the earth (or into your pot of earth) as an offering to the God and Goddess. As you do so, ask for their blessings upon the chalice.

Your other cup or chalice will contain the wine (or mead, or fruit juice, or water!) which is used at the end of your rite in the cakes and wine ceremony. Consecrate this when you come to do cakes and wine in the same way as you did for the water chalice, and pour some of the liquid to the earth - asking for the blessings of the God and Goddess upon the cup - before taking a sip yourself.

Cords, and any other items which you use in circle (eg, dish for the salt): place them upon your pentacle, and using your athame, draw a banishing Earth pentagram over them to purify them, and then an invoking Earth pentagram over them to consecrate (see Appendix B for pentagrams). As you trace the invoking pentagram, ask for the blessings of the God and Goddess on all the items upon the pentacle.

Scourge and sword: it is unlikely that anyone starting out in Wicca on their own will have either of these tools, and they are certainly not essential for solitary Wiccan practice. However, if you do happen to have either of these, the sword can be consecrated in the same way as the athame, and then used to re-cast the circle.

The scourge is a symbol of spirit, and its use is taught only within a coven. However, if you do have one, and wish to consecrate it, follow the instructions given for the consecration of the cords. We would briefly like to mention here that the scourge is perhaps one of the most misunderstood of all the Wiccan tools. It is NOT used in anger, punishment, sexual titillation, or in any dominating manner. It is the symbol of initiation, and of purification and enlightenment. However, some people feel that it is inappropriate within their own group, and have either replaced it with another symbol of purification and enlightenment, or simply dispensed with it. This is something which each individual must determine for themselves.

Finally - please remember that all the tools described above (and any others you choose to use) are exactly that - tools! They are designed to help you achieve your objective, but should never be mistaken for the objective itself. Always remember that the most powerful and effective tool you ever have is your own self.

CHAPTER FIVE

MAKING MAGIC

The practices of Wicca use techniques which are commonly called "magic". This might seem a little odd in a religion, until you consider the origin of the word "magic"; it is derived from magus, which is a term used to refer to members of an ancient Persian priesthood. It has been anglicised into mage, which is reckoned to mean both "a wise man" and "a magician" - one who practises magic. So, although today most people are generally unaware of the spiritual meaning of the word, there is nothing inconsistent with followers of a religion practising magic.

There have been many modern definitions of what the word means, mainly based upon Aleister Crowley's tenet that magic or as he spelt it, "magick" is "the Science and Art of causing Change to occur in conformity with Will." This should be understood in the context of Crowley's philosophy, which is that the magician's will operates through divine love.

Most modern commentators interpret Crowley's statement to mean that magic causes changes in human consciousness, which in turn, make changes in the external world. In other words, by changing the way we think about something, or by deliberately attempting to influence any matter, we will cause an actual physical change to occur in the world outside of our own self.

This is not such a strange concept if you accept the Wiccan belief that the entire universe is a living entity, and that changes in any part of it will necessarily cause other changes elsewhere. Rather like the laws of action and reaction: if John pushes Barbara, then she might well fall over; she will at least know that she has been pushed! That is an example of how magic works. Energy applied will cause a result. Not always the precise result that you were aiming for, but always some kind of reaction.

This philosophy is probably the oldest concept in magic and religion. It can be traced to mankind's earliest attempts to understand and influence the universe. Its pathway can be seen throughout all ancient cultures; it was passed to the scholars of the Renaissance, from whom the occult revivalists of the 19th and 20th centuries drew their inspiration, and is certainly fundamental to the philosophy of magic today. Modern science is gradually coming to realise that there is a subtle connection between all things - perhaps in the future they will also confirm what magicians and pagans have always known: that the human brain is also connected to the subtle energies of the universe!

Following this theory, the actual techniques of performing an act of magic become very simple. Firstly, you identify your objective, and then secondly, you set about influencing it. Of course it isn't quite that simple, although you'll be surprised how easy it is to, "cause changes to occur in conformity with (your) will."

There have been any number of books published about the techniques and practices of magic, many concerned with the types of magic performed by Wiccans. Any detailed discussion of these practices must fall outside the scope of this book, which is intended to provide a simple guide to the beginner. However, magic, no matter what its philosophical framework, is based upon a very few simple principles, which we can look at here, and refer readers to Appendix A for details of books which deal with specific techniques.

The most important thing to remember with any magical act is that it will only be effective if you are completely "in-tune" with the currents of the universe which you are trying to affect. As an analogy; imagine trying to switch on an electric light without being connected to any kind of power supply. You wouldn't get very far! Many people fail at their first attempts at magic simply because they are either unaware of the need to "plug-in" to the universal currents, or simply do not know how to go about doing it. You have to spend a considerable amount of time and effort making sure that you are "connected" to the power supply before you can hope to turn on the light, as it were. It is no use at all trying to influence the currents of the universe if you are not connected to them. This is one of the reasons why Wiccans spend so much time and energy simply attuning themselves to the rhythms of the Earth and the universe. Without that contact, we cannot hope to understand or influence what is happening around us.

Before our lives became artificially removed from the natural world, plugging in to the current was something that every human did unconsciously; either that, or they died! In the modern world most of us are removed from the seasons. We buy our food from the supermarket, and so have no need to understand the seasons as an integral part of our lives. It doesn't really matter to us whether food is "in season", for we are not concerned with its planting, nurturing or reaping.

In chapter 6 we will be looking at the Wheel of the Year in some detail, so will leave further discussion about "plugging-in" to the current till then. Just remember that if you want to perform any act of magic, spend time and effort first on making sure that you are aware of, and in tune with, the environment in which you live, and the greater world which surrounds us all. Most magical techniques emphasise the necessity of "raising power" in order to bring about desired results. This is a very simple phrase which refers to a very complex process - although the means used to "raise power" are generally fairly simple.

Wiccans are taught that there are eight ways of "making magic", or raising power. The most common ones are dancing and chanting, and these are the ones which we will discuss here. Dancing can mean anything, from a whirling dervish spin, to a sedate promenade! Most Wiccans meet in groups, and the circle dance, often accompanied by a chant or rune, nearly always follows the casting of the circle. Everyone present holds hands in a circle, and either walks, skips or runs, depending on the ability and fitness of those involved!

Wiccans believe that as our own energies are extended, so the common "cone of power" is created by the mingling of all the forces contained within the circle. Even if you work alone, you can still use dancing, or any kind of physical activity, to generate a feeling of power and energy within your circle.

Chanting is probably one of the most widespread of human activities, and is certainly found in one form or another in the practices of every religion. Wiccans use two main forms of chanting: the first is the repetition of a simple rhyme, or "rune", which states in very basic terms the purpose of the work in hand. An example is, "The Witches' Rune", written by Doreen Valiente. This has been published in many different books, and is one of the most commonly used chants in modern Wiccan circles. There are many, many others, and each group tends to have its own favourites. Books which contain examples of runes are given in Appendix A.

"Open" chanting - chanting which has no words, just sounds - is also commonly used, and is a very effective method of generating energy. It works best with a group of not less than four people. Sit in a circle facing inwards, and regulate your breathing until it is calm, deep and even. Then gradually allow an "aaah" sound to be made on each outward breath. Don't strain to keep the "aaah" going past your natural breathing rhythm. Stop when you need to draw breath again. The normal result of this is that as everyone has a slightly different breathing pattern, a continuous "aaah" begins to build around the group. As this grows, begin to be more deliberate about the sound you are making; it is no longer just a sound made by your outgoing breath, but an intentional vibratory hum. As the group continues to interweave the different patterns of sound, change your own vibration to an "eeeeh" or "owwwww", or one of the other vowels.

Vowel sounds create an outward flow of energy in an open manner; in other words, the sound is projected. The consonants tend to be more closed, and the feeling is one of cutting off the sound. Consonants which sound similar to vowels when chanted (b, c, d, g, p, t, v), and those for which you purse or close the lips (s, x, z), although different to the vowels, do have some similar energy patterns to them. These principles are used extensively in martial art, and are the basis of the Ki of Karate and Chi of Kung Fu, etc. Experiment by chanting these different letter sounds, and you will find that some extraordinary results will be achieved by this very simple process.

Other methods of raising power really fall outside of the scope of this book, and quite honestly, are not really essential to anyone beginning to practise Wicca. Dancing and chanting offer endless scope for the imaginative Wiccan, and it will be a long time before you run out of ideas based upon these two major techniques.

There are a few simple rules to remember whenever you attempt to perform any kind of magic. Firstly, there is only one "dictate" in Wicca, and that is, "Harm none, do what you will".

As a friend recently so rightly said: puts all of the Old Testament Commandments in six simple words! "Harm none" are of course the important words; not just avoiding the kinds of activities (including magic) which would deliberately hurt or upset another person, but also taking very great care when you do perform any act of magic, that you don't inadvertently harm someone. The best way to make sure of this is to carefully think through all the possible repercussions of any magical work you have planned. Then, when you word your request, or create the ritual, make sure that you include something along the lines of, "may this be for the best of all", or, "may none be harmed by my spell"; and most importantly, keep it firmly fixed in your mind that none are to be harmed by what you do. It's no good being half-hearted about anything in magic. If you want something badly enough, it is very easy to be less than careful about the fact that in the process of getting it, no-one should be hurt.

Secondly, don't use anything you don't understand. This may seem to be stating the obvious, but if we had a dollar for everyone we have heard of using ancient spells or formulas without having the least idea of what they're doing, we could both retire tomorrow! There are many magical "systems" in existence today, a number of them with a genuine tradition reaching back hundreds of years. Some modern magicians and Wiccans have a disturbing tendency of taking the bits and pieces of these systems that for some reason appeal to them, and then just ditching the rest. Rather like deciding you want to write in a foreign language, but without bothering with the grammar or punctuation.

Thirdly, all Wiccan magic should be performed under the blessing of the God and Goddess. If you are doing something which you feel the God and Goddess would not bless, then basically, you shouldn't be doing it.

Fourthly, keep it simple. The more elaborate, and the greater the number of supplementary activities you have to perform, the more chance you have of forgetting your words, or even worse, forgetting the whole purpose of the ritual.

Fifthly, if you use any items as a focus for ritual (eg, a fith fath, or some other item which is magically "charged") then make sure you take good care of it after the rite is over. A few years ago our coven used a fith fath (a small doll made from beeswax) as a focus for some healing for someone who had a growth on his leg. The ritual went very well indeed, and as usual, the fith fath was left on the altar overnight for maximum effect. Unfortunately, one of the cats got shut in the Temple, and was found the next morning throwing the fith fath around the floor, pouncing on it, and generally having a great time! We confessed our sin to our patient, and suggested that he resist going to safari parks for a while. Fortunately, his leg healed very quickly, and he avoided being mauled by cats! Seriously, this story is told as a cautionary tale, and the care of magically charged objects is very, very important.

One of the best ways of de-sensitising an object when its purpose is complete is to place it in salt water for the duration of one moon cycle (but obviously not if made from anything which will corrode if you want to re-use it at a later date). If you can afford to lose the object, and it is organic (and non-toxic) then placing it in the sea is a good means of returning everything back to its root element, and of course sea water acts as a purifying agent. Burning a magically charged object is also an option, although not one that we generally recommend without knowing all the details of its construction or purpose. Burning something sometimes has a negative influence, depending upon a number of factors, and should be used with care. However, as with all magic, it is your intent which is important, so there is no reason why you should not use fire to return an object to its root elements; just make sure that your intention is that, and not to "destroy" it.

Lastly, to return briefly to our comments about being connected to the universal currents; make sure that you perform your magic in accordance with the natural cycles. If you want something to grow, don't work your ritual at the time of the waning moon. If you want to start something new, aim to perform your ritual in the spring, and preferably at the time of the new moon. It isn't difficult to get yourself in tune with the turning of the seasons, and the phases of the Moon. We all have this ability naturally, but as we said above, continued dependence upon artificial environments has gradually eroded our awareness of how important the seasons are to us. Once you begin to tune-in to the real world (as opposed to the created, artificial one), you will instinctively know what are the right times to perform your magic. If you remove your magic from its natural environment, you will end up with an empty ritual - full of "meaning", but meaning nothing; and what's more, achieving nothing.

What sorts of things can be used in magic? Anything, basically. As we said earlier, the most powerful tool you have is your mind, but anything can be used to help as a focus of intent. There is also a complex theory of correspondences, which states that whilst all things are ultimately connected in some way, different substances or tools fall under the "rulership" of particular influences. This is a complex subject, for correspondences were first catalogued thousands of years ago, and have been amended and added to ad infinitum ever since. This results in a confusing, and often contradictory, set of correspondences, only some of which appear to make sense in today's world.

To give an example: in chapter 2 we mentioned that the athame is generally attributed to the element of air, but that an alternative, and very common attribution, is to fire. The chalice is consistently attributed to the water element - except where the chalice is what we term the "Holy Grail", or "Cauldron of Cerridwen", where the association is to the element of spirit, rather than water. To understand these attributions properly, you must remember that we are using symbolic language. We are not saying that the athame is air; simply that in our circle, or our philosophy, the athame represents air. William Blake put it beautifully: "Does the Eagle know what is in the pit, or wilt thou go ask the mole? Can wisdom be found in a silver rod, or love in a golden bowl?". Wisdom cannot be found in a silver rod (athame, or wand), but it can be represented to us by that symbol; similarly, love itself is not found in a golden bowl, but the symbolism of a golden bowl may be one of divine love.

The rulership of various substances is, as we mentioned above, complex and often contradictory. The best approach is to refer to a table of correspondences which seems to make the most sense to you personally, and then be guided by your own intuition. Refer to Appendix A for details of books which include standard tables of correspondences.

The attribution of colours to various rulers is also complex, and again, use whatever seems to make the most sense to you personally. We would like to point out that seemingly contradictory rulership of substances, tools or colours does not mean that the whole system of correspondences is useless. Modern Wiccans and magicians are in the enviable position of being able to draw upon the combined knowledge of thousands of years of mankind; knowledge which has been gathered since we first became sentient beings. A storehouse which contains infinite treasures, but, like Pandora's Box, can let loose a dreadful pestilence! A tendency of modern philosophy within the occult or mystery traditions is to attempt to reconcile many different techniques or skills into a cohesive whole. Sometimes that can work, but more often, a confusing conglomerate of very different philosophies is the result. Always remember that what makes perfect sense in its own location can be meaningless when transferred to another time or place.

It can also be difficult for the beginner to choose between two or more apparently authentic, and quite contradictory, colour or planetary rulership. Perhaps one from Babylon, another from Scandinavia and yet a third from the Mediterranean area. All three are likely to be "correct" within their own context, so as we said above, it is up to you to decide upon the set which seems to be most in-tune with your own understanding.

Having talked in some detail about the philosophy of magic, let's have a look at some of its practical applications. Let's imagine that you are trying to write an application for a job, and have decided that an appeal to Mercury may help you. Mercury is accorded influence over matters of communication, amongst other things. Your intent is focused, and you will have written into your ritual that you do not wish to harm anyone else by your actions. Now you feel that you want to support your mental approach with something physical, and so you search around for those things which are generally attributed to Mercury, and also check that time of your ritual is not during a period when the planet Mercury is "retrograde", or during the period of the waning Moon. If you must write your letter urgently, and cannot wait for the waxing phase of the Moon, then you could still perform your ritual, but it should be done during the morning in daylight hours, when the Moon's influence is weakest. However, there is no alternative to waiting for Mercury to go "direct" if you want to use the energies of this planet. (Retrograde and Direct are astrological terms which relate to the apparent motion of the planet. Many astrologers believe that the influence of any planet is diminished, or even distorted when it is retrograde. An ephemeris will give details of the motions of the planets, and a more detailed description of direct and retrograde motion will be found in any good book about astrology.)

You have read that dill is associated with Mercury, and as you have a dill plant growing in the garden, you cut a spray, which you place in a vase on your altar. You decide to use an incense which is made from gum mastic, the gum which many magical authorities seem to agree is associated with Mercury. You also have some lavender essential oil, and decide that after your bath or shower, you will anoint yourself with the oil. You have your normal coloured candles in each of the quarters, and have seen that Mercury's colour is often suggested as black and white, or yellow. As black and white seems to be more suggestive of writing (black lettering on white paper), you buy one black candle, and one white candle, and place them in candle holders side by side on your altar.

The purpose of the ritual is to help you write a letter of application, and you decide that you will actually write the letter inside the circle. So, unless you intend to just write out the draft copy in the circle, make sure that you have some good writing paper by your altar, and also that you have a decent pen with which to write. You are now ready to start your ritual. Make sure that you have done everything that needs to be done. Have your bath or shower, anoint yourself with the lavender oil, put on your robe if you are wearing one, and then cast your circle. (NB: light all the candles except the black and white ones; these will be lit later as a part of the ritual.)

After calling upon the God and Goddess to bring their blessings upon your work, sit before your altar, and think about what you need to write in your letter. After a short period of meditation, pick up the black candle in one hand, and the white candle in the other, and light them both simultaneously from the eastern quarter candle. You use the eastern candle because this is the place of the sunrise, and beginnings, and your letter aims to bring about a new job - i.e., a new beginning. Place the candles upon the altar, and resume your meditation. When you feel ready, start to write your letter. That is basically it. Very simple and straightforward, but from experience we can confirm that it is an effective ritual. When you have finished your letter (or the draft, if you are going to type it later), follow the instructions given in chapter 4 for cakes and wine and the closing the circle. If you had been performing candle magic, you would generally allow the candle(s) so used to burn out, rather than snuffing them. However, in this case, the candles were used as a support to the ritual, not its main focus, and so you could snuff them out when you extinguish the others.

This is a good point to mention candle magic, as it is certainly one of the most common, and most effective, types of magic used. The principles are very similar to those outlined above - you identify your objective, and then work your ritual using the relevant candle(s). These are generally chosen for their colour, and then magically charged by anointing and rubbing them with a suitable essential oil. Sometimes signs are also engraved upon the surface of the candle. From a simply practical point of view, it is better to use short, broad based candles than long thin ones.

As we mentioned above, with candle magic it is customary to let the candles burn out naturally, rather than snuffing them out. If you do this, make sure that your candles are not in either glass or pottery holders, which might shatter on contact with the flame, or wooden ones, which might catch on fire. We use an empty coffee tin part filled with sand, which provides a safe holder for the candle. This means that it can be left burning quite safely without us having to worry about it falling over and setting fire to the house! Even so, if we have to leave the candle burning in an empty house, we place the tin of sand in the bath or shower, and shut the door to the bathroom to keep inquisitive pets away.

Wiccan magic generally uses very basic items in its operation; not because it is "low" magic, or any other such silly description, but because Wiccans are generally very practical people, and adept at using whatever is available at the time. Wiccans also believe that everything in the universe is divine, and when you have a belief like that, it makes little difference whether the divine object you are using is a great silver chalice, or simple pottery cup. Wicca does not have a dogma which restricts its practitioners to an inflexible set of rules. It is a religion which above all else emphasises the importance of developing the self to become aware of the wider reality. It does not do this by imposing rigid observances, so if you want to use something which is unique to you, go ahead and do it.

Healing is something which Wiccans are often asked to do, and because most Wiccan circles are not open to outsiders, "absent" healing is the most common type. There are many ways of performing healing, so we will give an example here which is suitable for solo or group use. Directions are given for a group; for solo working, obviously ignore the bits which describe passing the chalice to another person.

You will need a chalice or cup of mineral water, with a quartz crystal submerged in the water. (It doesn't have to be mineral water, but avoid taking water from a tap, if you have a natural source of water which is safe to drink, by all means use that.) The crystal can be any shape or size, but from experience we can confirm that quartz gives the best results.

After the circle is cast, and the God and Goddess asked for their blessing upon the work, all sit in a circle facing the centre. The person who cast the circle fills the chalice with mineral/spring water, and places the crystal in the water. She/he then consecrates the water, (use the standard consecration of the water used for casting the circle), and then takes his/her place seated with the others. Each person holds the chalice for a period of meditation, where they visualise healing energy pouring into the chalice, using the crystal as a focus and battery for the energy. When everyone has done this, the chalice is placed at the centre of the circle, and everyone concentrates as a group on sending healing energy into the crystal. This can be silent meditation, or you can use chanting to help focus the intent.

When the chalice seems to be "full" with healing energy (one person should be responsible for "sensing" this) the chalice is returned to the altar. If possible, it should be covered with a cloth, and the water and crystal left in it overnight to continue charging. The next day, the water is decanted into a container which is then given or sent to the patient. We generally suggest that it is drunk, but we have also had success with the water being used to bathe a broken ankle. The crystal is only ever used for this one purpose, and when not in use is kept in a black bag. This helps to keep the crystal as a kind of healing battery, and makes sure that other influences don't disturb it.

This ritual works very well where the patient is known to you, but not present at the rite. Commonly, healing (even absent healing) relies upon some kind of link between the healer(s) and the patient. In this ritual, the link is the water in the chalice. However, if your group performs absent healing for people who are not known to you, and with whom you have no link, you can still use a form of the ritual described above. The difference is that when you sense that the chalice is full of healing energy, you visualise it being "sent out" to those who need healing. Some people "see" a shrouded figure take the chalice and walk away with it; others simply "see" the chalice levitate, and move off to do its work. When the chalice returns, you will find that it is "empty" of its healing power, and you know that your ritual has been successfully completed. You then pour the water onto the earth as a libation to the God and Goddess, thanking them for their help with your healing work.

There is one other healing ritual we would like to describe. This was created in 1986 by Julia and Rufus Harrington for a very specific purpose: to help Julia's father recover from a particularly bad attack of gastro-enteritis. It worked extremely well, curing in addition, a long-term heart condition, and has been used on several occasions since then, always with excellent results. It has also been used at Wiccan Workshops and Conferences in Britain and Australia, again with excellent results.

You will need a minimum of three people, and two different kinds of incense. Your censer should be a flat-bottom bowl which has been well-filled with sand, upon which sits a hot charcoal block to take the loose incense, or an incense cone if preferred. We give some suggestions in Chapter 7 about incenses that you could use, but would warn against using incense sticks, which are not suitable for this ritual.

The circle is cast in the usual manner, after which, the person who is to be healed, or is able to make a very strong link with the one who is to be healed ("Person C"), lies in the centre of the circle with their feet towards the south (or north, if the ritual takes place in the northern hemisphere). S/he is given as long as s/he needs to relax, and if acting as the conduit, to make the connection with the person for whom the healing is being performed. When s/he is ready, s/he raises his/her arm slightly, and the ritual begins.

Person A places the first bowl of incense upon the solar plexus of person C, who then immediately begins to visualise the illness leaving his/her body (or his/her contact's body) and passing into the incense. When person C feels that the illness has departed, s/he raises his/her arm. Person A then steps forward, and removes the censer from C's solar plexus. At this point, the ritual can take different forms, depending upon the number of participants. If there are three people, Person A holds the censer, and walks widdershins around the circle several times in a spiral pattern, until they arrive at the southern (northern in the northern hemisphere) quarter. Person B opens a gateway in the circle, and person A steps outside with the censer, and places it safely on the floor.

Person B has been waiting outside the circle, and now takes a second censer, upon which is placed a different incense, designed for healing. This is brought into the circle through the gateway, which is then closed by Person A, after stepping back inside themselves. Person B carries the censer deosil around the circle, re-tracing the spiral trod by Person A. When B reaches person C at the centre, he/she places the censer upon C's solar plexus. Person C then begins to visualise healing energy passing into their body from the incense. Once again, C raises an arm to indicate when s/he has completed this part of the ritual. The censer is removed from the solar plexus by Person B, and moving in a deosil direction, is placed upon the altar.

The person who has been the focus of the rite must be given some time to "ground", as we have found that they are often disorientated after the working, and need to relax, and eat and drink something before they come back to a normal waking state.

There are a number of variations upon this ritual. If you have more than three people, the censers can be passed from person to person in a circle or spiral formation, rather than one person walking a spiral. The format is the same; the illness is passed widdershins, and then taken out of the circle. The good health is brought in, and then passed deosil. There is an old Saxon healing rune which is often used by Wiccans, and is appropriate to chant in this rite as the second censer is being passed around. It is:

"This is the spell that we intone, flesh to flesh and bone to bone. Sinew to sinew and vein to vein, each one to its own again" (or, "each one shall be whole again" - both versions are used).

The original was used to heal the broken leg of a horse, but as many Wiccans will confirm, it is powerful in almost any case of illness. After the ritual is over, you need to dispose of the contents of the two censers. We generally dig a small hole in the earth, and return everything to the Great Mother, where it is transformed to its natural state. This is important - you are never "banishing" anything; merely moving it from one place to another. The energies which caused the illness were merely displaced from their natural state. They were not "evil" in themselves, and should not be treated as such. If you live near the sea, or by a river, you can of course throw the contents into the water, as the censer contains nothing but sand and organic matter. One word of warning to Australians: the charcoal remains hot for quite a long time, and if you dispose of it in the bush, make sure it is well

buried in the earth. You don't want to heal someone, only to cause a
bush fire in the process!

Talismans and amulets are often referred to in books about magic, and
many Wiccans have one or more of both in their possession. A
talisman is something which has been created for a specific purpose,
and is ritually "born and consecrated" in a circle. Many of the modern
talisman designs and techniques derive from a very famous grimoire
called, "The Key of Solomon"; which, incidentally, is also the source
of a number of the magical techniques which are commonly found in
Wiccan rituals.

Talismans can be created for almost any purpose, but are generally
used for something specific. Amulets are rather more general, and are
used to encourage luck, health, wealth, strength of purpose, etc. We'll
look at talismans first, and then deal with amulets later. Talismans are
often drawn in ink upon plain paper, but can also be embroidered upon
fabric, painted, engraved, carved - in fact, almost anything will make
an effective talisman. The talismans described in the Key of Solomon
and other similar grimoires generally use Hebrew letters for any names
which are used, and designs which are called sigils, or signatures,
relating to various planetary or elemental entities which the talisman
hopes to contact.

In Wicca, we would always include on our talisman a symbol of the
God and Goddess, under whose auspices all our work is performed,
and then would add symbols which we hope will plug us in to the
appropriate part of the cosmic energy network. Let's take a very simple
example: you have been feeling very tired, and drained of energy, and
so want to construct a talisman to give you energy. You read about the
different kinds of energy which each of the planets is said to generate,
and decide that either the Sun or Mars would be appropriate. As Mars
is also associated with war and aggression however, you decide that
the Sun would probably be best for your purpose.

Colours of the Sun are mostly golds and golden yellows, so you buy a gold candle to use as your altar candle, and find some gold coloured ink which you can use to draw your talisman. You read that Frankincense is attributed to the Sun, and so decide to use that as your incense. You look around, and notice a bush covered in bright yellow flowers, and so you cut a small spray to place upon your altar. While you were reading through the tables of correspondences you noticed that SUNday is under the rulership of the Sun, and so you decide you work your ritual on the first Sunday after the New Moon. That way, all the natural energies will be in your favour: it is spring, and so the Sun itself is growing in power; it is during the waxing phase of the Moon, and you are working your ritual on the Sun's own day. To complete the pattern of positive energies in your favour, make sure you start and finish your rite before mid-day, so that you are working with the rising Sun, not with the setting Sun.

Set up your working area as described in chapter 3, and make sure that you also have your gold ink, a pen or brush, and the paper on which to draw the talisman. In addition, you will need your cord, and a piece of cloth, preferably black, large enough to wrap the talisman (a large handkerchief size should be fine).

Cast the circle in the usual way, and call upon the God and Goddess to bless your work. Now take the blank piece of paper, and carefully draw the signs which you have decided to use. There is no need to make a talisman a work of art, but you should take care to draw the signs clearly and neatly, and try to make sure that you end up with a pleasing appearance. Figure 4 below is an example of the sort of thing you could do:

When you are satisfied with the talisman and the ink has dried, you need to exorcise it so that any unwanted (ie, non-solar) influences can be removed. Hold the talisman in one hand, and your athame in the other: describe a banishing earth pentagram (see Appendix B) in the air over the talisman saying as you do: "I cast out from thee all ills and impurities."

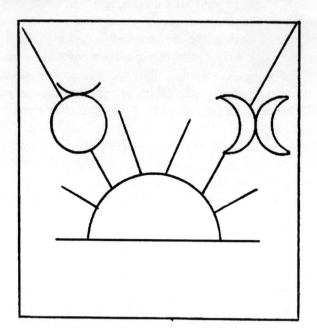

Fig 4.

Now carefully fold the paper in half, and then in half again. Wrap it in the cloth, and tie it with the cord. Take care not to bend the talisman as you do so. Symbolically you now have something which is pure, and is waiting to be given "life". Place the talisman, still bound in its cloth, upon the altar, and sit before it, thinking about the effect that you want it to have. When you feel that you have meditated upon this for long enough, pick up the talisman once more, and face east. Show the wrapped and bound talisman to the Air Guardian, and then move to the north (south). Again, show the wrapped and bound talisman, this time to the Fire Guardian, and then move to the west.

Repeat the process to both Water and Earth Guardians, and then take the talisman and sit at the centre of your circle, facing the altar. Using whatever method seems most appropriate - we would suggest chanting - "raise power", and sense this filling and surrounding your talisman.

Now slowly undo the cord which binds the cloth; as you do this, imagine that you are "giving birth" to the talisman. As you unwrap the cloth which covers it, feel yourself giving life to the talisman, and be aware of its potential energy. Now approach the altar, and carefully drip one or two drops of salt/water onto the talisman, taking care not to make the ink run. Now pass it through the incense smoke, and quickly over the top of the candle flame (take care not to let the flame touch the paper, though!). As you consecrate the talisman with the four elements in this way, remember that you are giving it life, and creating something which is balanced and pure.

Now ask for the God and Goddess to place their blessings upon your talisman, and imbue it with their divine love. Take it once more to the east, and repeat the process explained above of showing the talisman to each of the four Guardians. This time though, you are asking for their blessings upon it. Finally place the talisman upon the altar, and conclude your ritual in the way described in chapter 4, with cakes and wine, and the closing of the circle.

Take the talisman with you when you leave the circle, and immediately place it somewhere safe where it can continue to do its work. A pocket, wallet or purse is fine, or if you prefer, keep it under your pillow, where it can continue to cast its influence upon you while you sleep. Talismans should generally have an allotted time period for their existence - although we know of some that were created years ago for long-term purposes, and are still as effective today as they were then. However, it is a good idea, especially when you first start working with talismans, to give them a time span, and then ritually release the energies at the end of that period.

The best way to do this is, of course, in a circle. Cast in the usual way, and call upon the God and Goddess to bless your work. Have the talisman on the altar whilst you raise power in some way (probably chanting would be best). Then take the talisman, and hold it aloft at the centre of your circle (facing east), and thank the God and Goddess for their blessings upon the talisman. Then go to each of the Quarter guardians, starting in the east (then north, west and finally south), and thank each of them for their blessings. In the northern hemisphere of course, you would move east, south, west, north.

You now need to release the energies which were contained in the talisman. Hold the talisman in one hand, take your athame, and use it to describe a banishing earth pentagram (see Appendix B) in the air over the talisman. As you do say: "May all energies contained within this talisman be returned to their place in the universe, in peace and harmony." There are a number of ways of disposing of a talisman after this. Basically, as you have now "de-consecrated" it, it becomes nothing more than a piece of paper on which are written some symbols.

However, the reality is that you still have a charged item there, and it is best completely to return it to its constituent parts. We nearly always set fire to a talisman when it has fulfilled its purpose. We use a cast iron cauldron, but any flame-proof bowl will suffice. Keeping firmly in your mind the thought that you are now returning the elements of the talisman to their own places, light the paper from one of the altar candles, and then drop it in the bowl to burn out. When they are cool, scatter the ashes in your garden, or any outdoor place which is suitable.

Amulets are usually of a more general nature than talismans. They are commonly something like a piece of jewellery, or some other object which is either worn, or kept in the home/at work. To consecrate an amulet, you follow basically the same procedure as for a talisman. The important phases are: to exorcise any unwanted influences from it; wrap and bind it; show it to the four Quarter Guardians; energise it, and give it life (by removing its bindings and cover); ask for the blessings of the God and Goddess upon it, and then ask for the blessings of each quarter Guardian in turn. Keep in mind throughout the ritual what purpose you want your amulet to serve.

If you would prefer something more simple, you could just consecrate an amulet, following the instructions given in chapter 4 for the consecration of the cords. However, if it is to serve a specific purpose (eg, healing, energy, good fortune, etc.) then we would recommend that you use the talisman ritual, as it is much more effective.

The last type of magic we want to talk about here is cord magic. We mentioned one use of your cord in the ritual for creating a talisman, but there are many others. The most common is probably that which uses knots in the cord, the number of knots varying depending upon the aim of the ritual. Many covens use nine knots, as that number is associated with the Moon, and with the practice of Witchcraft. Three is also a commonly used number, as are seven, ten, and thirteen. A "knot spell" is often chanted as the knots are tied, and as with most Wiccan chants, there are many variations, although all aim for simplicity.

Cast your circle in the normal way, and after calling upon the God and Goddess to bless your work, take your cord(s), and sit at the centre of your circle. If you are working in a group, seat yourselves in a circle facing the centre. You can either perform cord magic individually, or have a common group aim, but obviously this has to be sorted out beforehand. You need to raise power for cord magic, which can be done in a number of ways. Here are some suggestions for groups: you can have the cords at the centre of the circle and all holding hands, dance around them, sending energy into them as you go. You can perform a "wheel dance", where each end of the cords is held by opposing dancers, forming a "cartwheel" shape. As you dance around, the cords become energised. Or, you can all sit on the ground in a circle, and have one cord per two people, who each hold one end, and gently pull against each other. The tension causes the cord to become energised.

Whatever form of energising you use, when you feel that the cord or cords are sufficiently charged, tie the desired number of knots, evenly spaced throughout the length of the cord. If you want to chant as you tie the knots, you could use something like this version of the 9-knot rune:

By knot of 1 my spell's begun
By knot of 2 my spell come true
By knot of 3 So Mote it Be
By knot of 4 open the door
By knot of 5 my spell's alive
By knot of 6 my spell I fix
By knot of 7 on Earth as in Heaven
By knot of 8 the stroke of fate
By knot of 9 this thing BE MINE!

When you have tied the final knot, spend some time in meditation, thinking about whatever it is you wish to influence, and then on a pre-arranged sign from the officiating group leader, all let go of the cords. They should be carefully collected up, wrapped in a cloth (or as we do, placed in a cauldron) for one lunar cycle. So, if you performed your ritual at the New Moon in November, then you would keep the cords wrapped up until the New Moon in December. If you wish to keep the knots for longer - for example, a spell which you wish to continue for several months - then by all means do so, but make sure that the cords are kept somewhere safe.

When you need to untie the knots, you follow exactly the same procedure as above, but where you tied the knots before, now you untie them. It is not common for anything to be said or chanted as the knots are untied, but the God and Goddess are always thanked for their help as the final knot is undone. A word of warning - if you pull on the cords during raising power, the knots can be very difficult to untie, but you have to persevere! Eventually even the tightest knot gives way.

There are many other forms of Wiccan magic, but to include them all would take an encyclopaedia! A few more have been included in Chapter 7, A Book of Shadows, and we suggest that you refer to the books listed in Appendix A for further ideas. Always remember that the ritual you create yourself will be the most effective.

CHAPTER SIX

THE WHEEL OF THE YEAR

The Wheel of the Year is of great significance to Wiccans, and is one of the principal keys to understanding the religion. As we said earlier, Wicca sees a profound relationship between humanity and the environment; for a Wiccan, all of nature is a manifestation of the divine and so we celebrate the turning seasons as the changing faces of our gods.

The Wheel of the Year is a continuing cycle of life, death and rebirth. Thus the Wheel reflects both the natural passage of life in the world around us, as well as revealing our own connection with the greater world. To a Wiccan, all of creation is divine, and by realising how we are connected to the turning of the seasons and to the natural world, we come to a deeper understanding of the ways in which we are connected to the God and Goddess. So when we celebrate our seasonal rites, we draw the symbolism that we use from the natural world and from our own lives, thus attempting to unite the essential identity that underlies all things.

Undoubtedly the significance of the Festivals has changed over the centuries, and it is very difficult for us today to imagine the joy and relief that must have accompanied the successful grain harvest. What with factory-farming, fast-freezing and world-wide distribution, our lives no longer depend upon such things and as a consequence, our respect for the land has diminished in proportion to our personal contact with it.

Wiccans believe that we can re-affirm this contact by our observance of the passage of the seasons, in which we see reflected our own lives, and the lives of our gods. Whether we choose to contact those forces through silent and solitary meditation, or experience the time of year in a wild place, or gather with friends in a suburban living room, we are all performing our own ritual to the Old Ones, and reaching out once more towards the hidden forces which surround us all.

What is of the utmost importance with the Wheel of the Year is that we understand what we hope to achieve through our festival celebrations, and avoid the trap of going through empty motions, repeating words from a book which may sound dramatic, but have no relevance in our everyday lives. That simply leads to the creation of a dogma, and not a living, breathing religion. It is not enough to stand in a circle on a specific day, and "invoke" forces of nature; those forces are currents which flow continuously throughout our lives, not just eight times a year, and if we choose not to acknowledge them in our everyday lives, there is little point on calling upon them for one day!

By following the Wiccan religion you are affirming your belief in the sanctity of the Earth, and acknowledging that you depend upon the Earth for your very life. Although modern lifestyles do not encourage awareness of our personal relationship with the turning seasons, or the patterns of life, growth, death and decay, that does not mean that they no longer exist. The ebb and flow of the Earth's energies may be hidden beneath a physical shell of tarmac and concrete, and a psychic one of human indifference, but they are nevertheless there for those who wish to acknowledge them once more.

We do this by observing the changes of the seasons, and feeling the changes reflected in our own innermost selves, and in our everyday lives. In our rituals we focus upon different aspects of the God and Goddess, and participate in the celebration of their mysteries; thus we re-affirm our connections on the most profound levels.

The Wiccan Wheel has two great inspirations; it is both a wheel of celebration, and a wheel of initiation. As a wheel of initiation it hopes to guide those who tread its pathway towards an understanding of the mysteries of life and the universe, expressed through the teachings of the Old Ones made manifest in the turning of the seasons. For a Wiccan, the gods and nature are one; humanity is a part of nature, thus humanity and the gods are one. In exploring the mysteries of the seasons we are seeking to penetrate more deeply the mysteries of the God and Goddess.

As a wheel of celebration, Wiccans accord to the words of the Charge of the Goddess, where She says, "Let my worship be within the heart that rejoiceth, for behold, all acts of Love and Pleasure are my rituals"; and that, "Ye shall dance, sing, feast, make music and love, all in my praise". Anyone can celebrate the turning of the seasons, in their own way, and in their own time. Wiccan covens will commonly gather together, and make the Festivals times of joyful merrymaking, but you can just as easily make the celebration a solitary one, or with just one or two friends. The principles do not alter; just the way in which you acknowledge them.

Wiccans generally celebrate eight Festivals, roughly six weeks apart, which are pivotal points in the solar (seasonal) cycle. Four of the Festivals are called the Lesser Sabbats: these are the Spring and Autumn Equinoxes, and the Winter and Summer Solstices. The other four Festivals are called the Greater Sabbats, and relate to particular seasons when in bygone days, certain activities would have been undertaken, usually followed by a party of some kind. There are variations upon the names by which these Greater Sabbats are known, but the simple ones are Candlemas, Beltane, Lammas and Samhain. We look at these in more detail in Chapter 7.

It is important to understand that the Festivals are celebrating a time of year: a season, not a date. Most books written about Wicca have been written by an author living and working in the northern hemisphere, who may quite rightly say that, "Beltane is celebrated on May Eve". Northern hemisphere readers will automatically interpret this as, "Beltane is celebrated at the end of spring, just before summer gets under way". In the Wiccan Book of Shadows, the poem by Kipling is used at this Festival which says, "O do not tell the Priests of our art, for they would call it sin; but we've been out in the woods all night, a' conjurin' summer in...".

Of course, "May Eve" in the southern hemisphere is autumn heading into winter; entirely the wrong time of year to celebrate the portent of summer. In much the same way, Christmas and Easter are celebrated at the wrong time of year in the southern hemisphere. In the Christian calendar, Christmas coincides with the Winter Solstice - and the growing popularity in Australia of the June Yule Fest, held in the Blue Mountains in NSW each year suggests an awareness of this, even if it is, in this case, expressed in a commercial sense.

The date of Easter changes each year, because it is celebrated upon the first Sunday after the first Full moon after the Spring Equinox (and they try to tell us that Easter wasn't originally a Pagan Festival!). So in the southern hemisphere, according to the rules by which the date of Easter is determined, it should fall sometime in late September or early October each year. However, Christianity is not a religion which sees a particular connection between humanity and the environment, and therefore has no problem in celebrating Easter in autumn, and Christmas at the Summer Solstice. Wicca is different though, and it IS important to us to attune ourselves to the passage of the seasons, hence we follow the natural cycle wherever we live. Beltane falls at the start of summer; therefore in the southern hemisphere, this means celebrating our Beltane rite at the beginning of November, not the beginning of May.

The Wiccan Wheel of the Year is precisely that: a wheel. It is a continuous circle of life, death and rebirth as one season follows another. It is not simply a disconnected collection of dates, upon which rituals taken from a Book of Shadows are performed. The whole key to understanding the Wiccan philosophy can be found within the Wheel of the Year, as we learn how one phase of life proceeds from another.

The Wiccan year starts and finishes with Samhain, which is also known as Hallowe'en, or All Saints Eve. It is the celebration which falls just before the dark nights of winter take hold. The Winter Solstice comes next, where Wiccans celebrate the re-birth of the Sun; at Candlemas, about 6 weeks later, we celebrate the first signs of the growing light (longer days), and of spring beginning to show itself. The Spring Equinox follows, and is the time when day and night are equal in length, and the Sun is on its increase. Next is Beltane, herald of summer, and the Festival where Wiccans dance around a tree, crowned with a garland of spring flowers, and decked with red and white ribbons.

About six weeks after Beltane we come to the Summer Solstice, when the Sun reaches its greatest height, and we have the longest day/shortest night. Then the Sun begins its way back down towards winter, but we are still in summer. Six weeks after the Solstice is Lammas; in agricultural societies, this would not have been such a definite "six weeks", as it actually marks the end of the main harvest, where we receive the benefits from our hard work.

The Autumn Equinox follows, again about six weeks later, and is often celebrated as a Harvest Festival. The next Festival, some six weeks after the Equinox, is Samhain, which is the time just before the winter really sets in, and when food is stored, and we remember those who have passed away. In many countries this is the time when the Lord of the Wild Hunt rides, which is mirrored in the way that the winds are often wild at this time of year, and the clouds ragged and wind-torn.

In different parts of the world (even within a single country), the seasonal aspects can vary significantly, but generally speaking, you should be able to feel the change from winter to spring; spring to summer; summer to autumn and then autumn to winter. The specifics will change, but the general trend is very similar - one season leading to another. You have only to become aware of the natural changes in your own environment to realise that the concepts of the Wheel of the Year are valid wherever you may be.

As a Wheel of initiation, the Wheel of the Year is the path which leads us through the experiences of our gods towards that point which Jungian psychologists call individuation, and which Wiccans call knowledge of the Old Ones. As with all mystical experiences, these mysteries are not communicated in an academic or intellectual manner; they are direct experiences which each individual shares with the Old Gods. Different traditions have developed different ways of travelling the Wheel, but all ways have a common purpose, and all are equally valid, provided the basic principles are sound.

Let us have a look at the Wheel of the Year in more detail, using for our framework a mythology which is used by our own Coven. It is based upon the Gardnerian and Alexandrian traditions in which we were initiated, but has evolved over several years, and has been greatly modified to reflect our own understanding of the turning wheel of the seasons.

We should say at this point that we use the terms "King" and "Queen" to refer to the principle characters in the mythology. It is important to understand that we are not referring to a modern monarchy, but to the ancient Pagan principles those titles infer. In this mythology, the King is the priest/king of the forest: his tale is told in many forms in many lands. He is the essential male that lies within all men, and is the animus (in its Jungian sense) of all women. The Queen is Sovereignty: she is the mysterious soul of nature; the essential woman that lies within all women, and is the anima of all men.

So to begin our journey: how do we set out to explore the mysteries of existence? Well, the journey begins with a question - we have first to be aware that there is a mystery to explore! And that most basic of questions is: "where did life come from? how did it all begin?". For a Wiccan there is an underlying spiritual intuition that the answer to that question is quite simply that the universe was created by deity. So we celebrate the beginning of the Wheel of the Year as being the creation of all life by the God and the Goddess; we begin with a creation myth.

The Wheel of the Year starts with Samhain; at this time we celebrate the Great Rite - the joyful union of the God and Goddess in the Otherworld. This touches the very depths of the mystery. We celebrate at this time the conception that will lead to the birth of all creation.

Wiccans celebrate all life as a manifestation of the mystery of the gods, but do not pretend to understand how such life came into being. Nor do we claim to fully understand our gods; to the Wicca they are a mystery, and when describing our vision of deity we use symbols to express as best we can the vision we have seen. We do not know how the universe was created and this remains essentially mysterious. However, by choosing to take the path of initiation - that is, by following the Wheel of the Year - we can learn to commune more deeply with the gods, and experience visions which can reveal a little of the mystery.

The vision that we have of Samhain is of the creation. In the Wicca the inexpressible mystery of the deity is symbolised in the form of the God and Goddess. Thus at Samhain we celebrate their love as the root of all creation. Samhain is the time of creation: the moment when life is conceived in the womb of the Great Mother.

As we proceed to the next of the festivals - Yule - it should not be surprising to find that following the moment of conception we should seek to understand the moment of birth. The conception, the moment of creation deep within the mystery, took place at Samhain. The seed planted at this time gestates in the womb of the Goddess until the child of the gods - in essence, the whole of creation - emerges from the womb of the Great Mother. This is celebrated at Yule, which is symbolised by the birth of the Sun. In pre-Christian times, this time was called "Giuli", and followed "Modra Necht" - the Night of the Mothers.

Yule is celebrated at the time of the Midwinter Solstice. This is the time of the longest night, and of the shortest day. The Sun is seen to be symbolically born anew, as the Great Mother gives birth at the time of the darkest night. The Sun is a vitally important symbol to us, for it has long been known that all life on Earth is dependant upon the Sun. The

Wheel of the Year itself is based upon the solar cycle, and the Sun is seen as symbolic of the life force which we worship as the God and the Goddess. The Sun is the dominant force in all our lives. Without its light and heat, life as we understand it is impossible. The passage of the Sun through the heavens regulates the passage of the seasons we experience upon the Earth, and is therefore the foundation of the Wiccan Wheel of the Year.

At the Midwinter Solstice we celebrate the rebirth of the Sun. Many Wiccan covens follow the old Pagan tradition of enacting this as the Goddess giving birth to the Child of Promise. It was at the Midwinter Solstice in the northern hemisphere that the birth of Mithras was celebrated. For the same reason it was decided in 273 A.D. to appoint this date to celebrate the birth of Christ; the son (Sun?) of God.

In the world of nature, Yule signifies the moment of the rebirth of the Sun. In our own lives we can take it to represent the moment of physical birth. Thus in our ritual cycle, we enact the rebirth of the Sun by the lighting of candles, and especially the lighting of a flame within the cauldron to represent the emergence of new life from the darkness of the womb of the Goddess. In other words, we have our first glimmering of the mystery as it is made manifest upon the Earth. We ritually invoke the Great Mother and All-Father, and we symbolically enact the Goddess giving birth to the new year. In human terms the child represents all the potential for life, as yet unaware that all the mysteries of the universe lies hidden deep within. Like Adam and Eve in the Garden of Eden, the child is born in innocence, created in the image of the gods.

We have taken the second step upon our journey. From now on the days continue to lengthen as the Sun climbs towards its height at the Summer Solstice. In response to the greater heat of the Sun, the land begins to awaken as we start the journey from winter towards spring. The next festival is Imbolg, also known as Candlemas. As we might guess from the name given to it by the Christians, it is a festival of lights which celebrates the growth of the Sun. By Imbolg, the days are appreciably longer. Our understanding of this festival has been guided by ancient Pagan tradition and our own inspiration. We see this as a time of purification and most especially a time of initiation into the female mysteries. At Imbolg we observe in nature the awakening potential for the fullness of summer. In human terms we represent this by the first female menstruation. This is the virgin aspect of the Goddess, marking the awakening of her potential to become the mother.

We celebrate this ritual by arming the young virgin with the powers of the elements. We celebrate her initiation into the mysteries of her sex. To reflect this essential female mystery, we enact the young girl being instructed by her mother and grandmother into the mysteries of being a woman. Thus we reveal that the mystery of the virgin is also found within the mother and crone as well.

It is at Imbolg in many parts of Britain that the women of the house dress a sheaf of oats in woman's clothing, and lay it in a basket called "Brighid's bed". They also place a small phallic club in the bed and then call out three times, "Brighid is come, Brighid is welcome!", and leave candles burning all night beside the bed. Behind all this we catch glimpses of deeper mysteries that can only be grasped by passing beyond a mere intellectual appreciation of the symbolism.

To continue our journey we now come to the Spring Equinox. It might seem that celebrating Imbolg as a female mystery is rather unbalanced, but no; for reasons of tradition, and because woman reach puberty before men, it is not until the Spring Equinox that the initiatory male rite is enacted. In this we arm the young god with the knowledge of his own creative power; he is initiated into the mysteries of his sex, just as the young girl was armed with the powers of her potential. This ritual expresses the mystery that he contains within his young life; the potential to become a father and wise old man.

This continues to reflect the turning tide of the seasons. We are now in the spring. New life is awakening on all sides. The sap is rising in the trees, and both the young man and young girl have awakened to the mysteries of their sexuality. The Spring Equinox is a vital moment in the passage of the solar cycle. Day and night now stand equal, and from this point onwards the light will dominate the darkness. The long dark nights of winter have at last been overthrown.

Between the Spring Equinox and Beltane the young man and woman pursue one another, each becoming more aware of the other sex. Thus the man understands that there is more to the mystery of life than pure masculinity, and the woman sees that there is more to life than her femininity. Having found this vision, they express it in their desire to be joined as one.

We arrive now at Beltane. This is the time of the sacred marriage when the young man and woman are joined together as husband and wife. With their wish to be married, they have glimpsed that the mysteries of love may lead to a deeper union still - in essence, to a union with the gods. By going beyond their sense of individual self to embrace one another, they have taken a profound step toward the God and Goddess. They have discovered that deep within themselves they are both male and female, and the experience of this brings a new sense of joy and wholeness.

Beltane is a time of joy and celebration; the dark of winter is forgotten, and summer is coming. It is a time of fertility and fire. We dance the ancient mystery of the Maypole, celebrating our understanding of the mystery of love. The pole is crowned with a garland of flowers to symbolise the union of male and female; the ribbons are red and white, reminding us of menstrual blood and male sperm. The dance is the sexual fire, as we dance about the pole winding the ribbons in the pattern of the spiral, which reveals the mystery of the serpent; that ancient awakener who slumbers until warmed by the rising Sun.

This is the time of the sacred marriage. It is a moment when human consciousness has grasped the powers of nature, joined with those powers and shared in the mystery of life. The land and our lives are married as one. For those that are able to see it, there is a vision of the creation of all life by the God and the Goddess. For the mystery is now revealed for all to see - in seeking to integrate the male and female powers, the woman conceives of her husband. She is pregnant and will bear a child.

Through their union they discover their deeper selves, which we symbolise as the King and Queen of the land. The man and woman now take up their new roles, and rule the kingdom of their new found lives. At Imbolg and the Spring Equinox a man and a woman were instructed in the powers of nature. Now at Beltane that knowledge is transformed into understanding. For in joining together they have understood that their lives and the land are one.

The land continues to bring forth life in an ever greater profusion. The woman who is now the Queen begins to show the first signs of the Beltane seed planted in her womb by her husband, the King. So now we come to Midsummer, the height of the solar Wheel. This is the time of the longest day and shortest night, and a time of maturity, both in the agricultural cycle and the lives of the man and woman. They rule now as King and Queen; just as the Sun is at its height, so too they are at the height of their creative powers. The woman's mature power is reflected in her approaching motherhood. The man's power is reflected in his kingship, and in his mastery of nature and rule of the kingdom. Together the King and Queen preside over the kingdom of their lives, celebrating the vision of creative light.

But the light does not continue to rise. The vision of light must once more give way to a growing darkness. As things grow, so too they must wither and die. From Midsummer, the Sun must fall, until reborn once more at the Winter Solstice. Thus Midsummer is a celebration of the King and Queen's power, but must also reflect the returning current of darkness. We symbolise this by the appearance of a challenger who confronts the couple. Until now the King and Queen have ruled supreme; they have imposed their will upon their kingdom without challenge, but now a dark figure must appear. This is the beginning of the ancient pagan theme of the battle between the brothers; the light and dark kings now begin their conflict.

The challenger seeks to abduct the Queen; the child she bears represents the kingdom. The King must now defend the land. They fight, light against dark, but as yet the sun is still supreme, and the King drives the challenger back. But, the challenger is armed with the power of fate: we know that the Sun must fall. With a single stroke the challenger wounds the King, laying open his thigh; but still the light is the greater power, and the King defeats the challenger. The light still rules supreme, but a shadow has fallen over the kingdom.

Thus Midsummer comes to a close. The King and Queen remain at the height of their power, yet a new force - darkness - is awakening in the world. As the seasons continue to turn, the gods begin to reveal a further mystery: not only are they light, they are also dark as well. Thus the King and Queen have awakened to a deeper mystery; they have seen that not only are they male and female, but they are also light and dark as well.

As we look at the natural world, we see that the Sun is now waning. The days grow shorter, and we sense profound changes in the world around us. After Midsummer, the next festival is Lammas. The crops have matured, and in the way of nature, aged and turned to seed. The days are still longer than the nights; the light still rules in the land, but the powers of darkness are now visibly growing. Summer is coming to an end and we are approaching autumn. To symbolise the theme of the waning light and growing power of darkness, we celebrate Lammas by reaping the harvest; thus we celebrate the end of the vision of light. As we have sown, so now we reap, but in cutting the corn we signal the end of the cycle of growth.

As we gather in the harvest we watch as the power of the Sun wanes. The cutting of corn is an ancient symbol of death and transformation, and reflects the seasonal changes at work in the land around us. As we look to the King and Queen, who were married to the land at Beltane,

76

we see in their lives a reflection of these themes. Just as the harvest is reaped, so the Queen now births her child.

The mystery of Lammas is that by fulfilling the vision of light in bringing to fruition the seed sown in the spring, we must face the vision of death. For the King bears the wound he received at Midsummer; it is a wasting wound and will not heal. He slowly weakens, his creative power spent. He is still King, but his powers are waning, a reflection of the falling light. But Lammas is also a time of hope, for in the cutting of the corn the seed is gathered in, which is the hope for life to come. As the King looks to his first born son he looks to the heir of the kingdom. We celebrate Lammas as a time of fulfilment; it is a time of joy, when we reap all we have sown.

Both King and Queen have been transformed. The King had to accept the glimpse of the vision of death in his killing of the challenger and taking of a mortal wound; so now the Queen dies to herself, for in giving birth she has given the child a part of her life, passing her power to her son. As the Wheel of the Seasons turns, it reveals that the gods embrace both life and death. Just as the man and woman were born, so too they must die. Lammas brings the vision of mortality, but reveals the hope of the immortal spirit hidden in the new cut grain, made manifest in the new born child, who symbolises the awakening darkness; he is the power of the waning Sun. He emerges from the womb as the growing darkness appears in the natural world.

We must now move on. Time will stand still for no-one. The wheel must turn, and we must turn with it, as our lives reflect the turning cycle of the seasons. We must now make our way to the Autumn Equinox, where once again the powers of light and darkness stand as equals, but now it is the darkness that is in the ascendant.

It is the nature of human beings to resist the darkness. Humanity fears death above all things. It is the root of all our fears; death is the final initiation. Only through an acceptance and understanding of death can we hope to understand the gods. Only in accepting death can we truly accept life. Life and death are two sides of the same coin; we cannot have one without the other.

By the time we reach the Autumn Equinox, it becomes harder to describe the mysteries that we celebrate. The mystery that can be taught or explained is not, after all, a mystery. At the Autumn Equinox we must face life's greatest mystery: death. This is the hardest trial of all. In the ancient mystery schools, and in shamanic practices, the most important of initiations was - and is - the near death experience.

The child born at Lammas is now a young man. He is the reflection of the growing powers of darkness. The old King of Light bears his mortal wound and is now advancing in years, his powers waning as the days grow shorter, and the Sun falls lower and lower in the sky. The Queen also is no longer young; the flower of her youth is past. The King and Queen are ageing with the land, for they and the land are one.

But as is natural in human affairs we none of us want to admit the darkness. We fight against the coming of the night. So the King and Queen each in their own way try to hold onto the kingdom they have been at such pains to build. The King's powers are waning; his son is in the first flush of youth and vigour, and has been initiated into the mysteries of his power. The King grows weak, and must rely upon his son to defend the kingdom. But, the King now fears his son as a potential challenge to the throne. The Queen likewise does not want to relinquish her power. She sees that her husband grows weak and infirm, and is no match for a challenger. To maintain her position in the kingdom she relies on the power of her son.

Finally, in the dead of the night, the old pagan tale replays itself. The battle begun at the Midsummer Solstice between the light and darkness must now be resumed; the King and his son fight as the Equinox comes upon us. Sword against spear the battle rages; the experience of the King against the naked strength of his son's youth. The Queen watches as they fight, torn by hope and fear. But as they fight, there is a great mystery at work. Both the King and Queen now face their fear of death, and as they look death in the eye there is a moment of understanding. The King, the Queen, and the land are one. Thus they are both the light and darkness. In the moment of vision the King looks upon his son, and at last realises that he is only fighting himself, for all things are one. The King and his son understand the mystery, and they join in love as one. They give up the conflict of light and dark to pass beyond this world, and they become the Lord of the Otherworld. The Queen too has seen both life and death, and knows that they are one. With this realisation she becomes the Crone, and understands the ancient mystery. The Equinox marks her last menstrual cycle; she can no longer bear children.

So now we must take our last step upon the Wheel; we come at last to Samhain, from where it all began. As we saw at the beginning this is the Wiccan New Year. The Queen has become the Crone - the Hag, the Witch. She lives alone, for the King is now dead. The Sun is waning toward the Solstice; winter is upon us, and the night is now longer than the day.

If we look to the land, the cycle of growth has come to an end. The kingdom of the old year has symbolically passed away, transformed by the turning of the seasons. The Queen is now a Witch; the ancient hag crone who knows the mysteries of life and death. In making her journey she has discovered the ancient power which lies behind the Wheel of the Year. She has seen the spring, the summer, autumn and winter, and she knows that an ancient mystery lies hidden within it all.

Standing alone, for she is feared by those who have yet to walk the Wheel, she kindles the ancient Samhain fire. As she raises her arms in invocation to the Lord of the Otherworld, a great storm gathers. The veil is opened between the worlds. The storm breaks, and the Wild Hunt is upon us as the spirits of the dead are led from the Otherworld by the ancient Horned God; the Ancient Lord of the Samhain fire. To complete the final turn of the Wheel, the Crone must now go with him back into the Otherworld. She and the Horned Lord travel together

79

back into the depths of the mystery. There they join in love as one; the supreme moment of the true Great Rite in which all the mysteries of the male and female, all the mysteries of the light and dark are married together as one, as the seed is planted deep within the womb of the Great Mother.

For now in the natural cycle the seeds of nature fall to the ground, the seed of life to come. The seed harvested at Lammas is now planted in the earth, fulfilling the mystery of the return. For a while the land sleeps, and lies fallow. The darkness seems complete, but of course we know that we will eventually return to the Winter Solstice, and the cycle will continue.

Let us now approach the Wiccan Wheel of the Year as it is meant to be: as a mystery. Forget the intellect, and allow your intuition and emotions to be your guide. What follows is a guided visualisation, which you can read onto a tape, or have one person read aloud, as you follow the journey it describes. Allow the images to form naturally in your imagination, and you will find yourself making a magical journey through the mysteries of the gods.

For those who are not used to following a guided visualisation, there are a few simple rules to observe. Before starting any meditation work (which includes the kind of altered state that guided visualisation encourages), seat yourself comfortably in a quiet room, free from distractions. Take the phone off the hook, and tell anyone who lives with you not to disturb you. You can of course do this out of doors, but if you do, make sure you are well off the beaten track, with no danger of bush walkers stumbling over you, or any other kinds of disturbance. Have a pen and pad handy, and if it helps you to relax and focus, use some incense.

The Guided Visualisation:

Make sure you are seated comfortably, and spend a few moments quietly, allowing your mind and body to relax. Now, close your eyes, and allow these images to build in your imagination:

It is dark, and a chill wind is blowing. You are standing within a mighty forest, and can feel the ground hard and cold beneath your feet. You look up, and see the stars, but there is no Moon. Patiently, you wait. You hear a sound behind you, and turn and look over your shoulder. You realise that you are standing upon the edge of a clearing: at its centre burns a fire, with an old man seated before it. He is wearing tattered animal skins, and has long ragged hair which blows about in the wind. On the far side of the clearing you see the mouth of a cave, and standing before it is the mighty figure of the Horned God.

You turn back and look through the trees, looking towards the eastern horizon. For tonight is the longest night: the dark time before the Sun is reborn at the Winter Solstice, and you wait patiently for the first rays of the new born Sun. At last you see a faint glimmer of light upon the eastern horizon, and as the rays of the new born Sun rise in the morning sky, you hear the sound of a new born babe crying. You turn and look back across the clearing as an old woman walks out of the cave carrying a new born child in her arms. The Horned God reaches forwards and caresses the child's cheek, and then the old woman takes the child, and sits by the side of the old man at the camp fire.

As the Sun continues to rise in the sky, you know that you have witnessed a very great mystery - the mystery of birth - the birth of the Sun, and of the Son. You leave the clearing, and walk back through the forest to your own cottage, where you warm yourself at the fire, for you are chilled through after your long vigil throughout the darkest night.

Days pass, and although the ground is still hard and cold, and the nights long and dark, you are aware of a change in the season, and know that winter is drawing to its close. One night as you are about to go to bed, you hear a tinkling of bells from deep within the forest, and are strangely drawn towards their sound. As you make your way through the night, a waxing Moon lights your path, and at last you find yourself once more in the clearing. You look towards the cave, and see that a great red veil hangs across the mouth, and that the old Crone, and another woman stand before it. The other woman is younger than the Crone, but obviously not a youth, and you instinctively realise that this is the Crone's own daughter.

As you stand and watch you realise that the bells are being shaken by the Crone, and that she and her daughter are softly singing an ancient song: a song which calls to the Virgin to awaken, and to come forth as the herald of winter's end, and spring's beginning.

The two women reach up, and with a single movement, rend the veil, tearing it away, revealing the Virgin standing poised upon the threshold. She is purity and innocence: a young figure - naked and blindfold, carrying in her hands a posy of bright yellow flowers, symbolic of the growing powers of the Sun.

The Mother and Crone reach forward, and linking their hands behind the Virgin, they pull her out of the cave. They lead her towards the fire, and then the Mother speaks quietly to her. You see the Virgin nod. The Crone then seems to ask her a question, and although you cannot hear the answer, it seems she has spoken truly, for the Crone nods, and reaches up to remove the blindfold. The Virgin blinks her eyes, and stretches. She begins to dance slowly around the fire at the centre of the clearing, full of the joy of her awakening, and in the knowledge of her power and potential as a woman.

Self-contained, she dances the dance of life; of blood and waters flowing freely, no longer frozen and still. You turn and leave the clearing, taking one last look at the Virgin dancing joyfully around the fire. As you walk back through the forest, you feel an answering power moving through the land, and you are aware that the Earth is beginning to come alive beneath your feet, and on the trees you see the yellow blooms which are the promise of spring, and the end of winter.

Day by day the Sun now grows visibly stronger: the land has awakened from its sleep with the fire dance of the Virgin, and now the Sun itself approaches the magical time of the Equinox: the time when day and night are equal, but when light is in the ascendant. The day of the Equinox dawns bright and clear. The wind is fresh, and all around you are signs of spring. From deep within the forest you hear the sound of a horn, and deep within your innermost self you are aware of a stirring response to its call. You make your way quickly through the forest; as you approach the clearing, you realise that you are not alone, for all the creatures of the forest are gathered upon the edge of the clearing. They too have answered the summons of the horn.

At the centre of the clearing stands a naked young man, his skin shining with reflected sunlight. He is blindfold: before him stands the old man, and behind him, the mighty figure of the Horned God. It was he who blew the horn. The old man dances around the youth - slowly, a shambling kind of dance - shaking a rattle and chanting softly. He stops. The Horned God whispers to the youth, who nods his head in reply. The old man then asks the youth a question, and after listening to the reply, nods, and reaches up and removes the blindfold. The youth blinks, and stretches. The Horned God hands him the horn. He puts this to his lips, and a single blast echoes through the forest. With a laugh the youth leaps away into the forest, followed by all the birds and animals, for he is Lord of the Forest. You feel a stirring in your own blood, and before you realise what has happened, you find yourself chasing the figure of the youth on his mad dash through the forest. It is a wild and carefree dance, and you feel the answering echo from the trees, and from the Earth, as they are warmed by the growing Sun. The Land and the Youth both awaken to their fertile potential.

As you run through the trees, out of the corner of your eye you see a flicker of white; you turn, and there hidden in the trees you see the Virgin, watching and waiting. She is looking curiously at the Lord of the Forest, intrigued by his strength and drawn by his beauty. He sees her watching, but on this day, he is too full with the joy of being in control of his own creative power to cease his headlong chase through the forest. Gradually you tire, and at last you find yourself walking back through the forest to your own cottage, where you find rest.

All through the growing spring the Virgin and the Young Lord watch each other through the forest. Each aware of the other, but both self-fulfilled with their own potential and power. But the Sun keeps getting stronger, and at last we come to that moment where the Young Lord and the Virgin realise that they have a greater destiny to fulfil, and driven by their natural desires, and the signs of the burgeoning world all around them, they seek each other out, and in celebration of the great mystery of the Land Marriage, they join as one.

It is the height of spring, and the signs of fertility are all around. As you make your own way towards the clearing, you feel the warm Sun upon your face, and feel the life in the Earth beneath your feet. In the centre of the clearing stands a great tree trunk, crowned with a garland of spring flowers, with many red and white ribbons fluttering in the breeze. From far and wide people have travelled to the clearing, for today is the day of celebrating the growing Sun, and the fertile Earth. Men and women take hold of the ribbons, and enact their own celebration of Life as they dance the pattern of the sacred spiral of creation around the tree. You hold your ribbon firmly, and watch the spiral form as you dance the ancient steps that have been danced since first Man and Woman were joined as one.

You hear cheering and shouts of laughter, and there, walking through the crowd hand in hand come the Young Lord and his wife - Virgin no longer. Together they have celebrated the sacred mystery in accordance with the Old Laws: for they have joined in love, and so have become the King and Queen of the Land.

And the weeks pass, and the Sun grows ever stronger in the sky, and the King grows in strength and majesty. The Queen begins to show signs of her pregnancy, the mirror of the crops and fruits that the Land begins to produce, for the Queen represents the Land, and is at one with it.

At last the day arrives when the Sun reaches its most powerful time: the Midsummer Solstice. The King and Queen are at their peak too, reflected in the majesty of the King, and the growing life in the womb of the Queen. To mark this day, the King and Queen host a great celebration in the forest clearing: a feast to mark the Solstice day, and their own creative powers which have brought many good things to the Land. All day the feast and games continue, with the King and Queen bestowing their blessings upon everyone.

At long last the Sun begins to sink slowly towards the west; as it falls you hear a disturbance upon the edge of the clearing. You see people running, and hear their screams. And then into the clearing stalks a dark figure, his black cloak swirling around him, wearing a helmet which obscures his face from view - shadow of darkness in the forest. He strides towards the King, and in a loud clear voice, challenges him for the right to rule the kingdom, and for the Queen as his consort.

The King must protect what he has striven so hard to create, and must protect his wife and unborn child. He accepts the challenge, and a great battle ensues as the Sun slowly sinks in the west. The challenger lays the King's thigh open with a sweep of his sword, but is unbalanced, and despite his wound, the King manages to throw the challenger to the ground and disarm him. The challenger begs for mercy, but the King fears this dark and threatening figure, and so ignoring his cries for mercy, he plunges his sword deep into the challenger's heart. And so in order to protect, the King destroys, and a shadow of darkness is cast upon the Land. The challenger's blood soaks into the Earth, and the Sun finally sinks beyond the western horizon.

You make your way back to your cottage, as the King is carried away to have his wound dressed. The next day the Sun rises as before, and seems as strong as it ever was, but you have seen and felt the shadow of the dark, and now sense a change in the Land. Instead of growing, things are ripening; the heat of the summer Sun brings the crops and fruit to ripeness, but the growth is now over. And just as the Land gives forth its fruits, so now does the Queen give birth to her son. The wheat is harvested; the barley made into ale; and a great feast is held to give thanks for all the good things of the Earth, and for the safe birth of the King and Queen's son.

But in giving birth, the Queen is no longer simply a wife; she becomes the Mother. She knows that her son is the hope for the Land, for the King's wound, taken at the Midsummer battle, is a wasting wound, and will not heal. He grows weaker by the day, a reflection of the waning powers of the Sun. The Queen knows this, and as her son grows, she trains him in the ways of sovereignty. The King sees only that his son grows stronger, as he grows weaker. He watches the Sun wane day by day as summer slips towards the time of the Equinox, when once again day and night are equal; but this time, the dark is in the ascendant.

At last the night of the Equinox arrives. The King feels drawn towards the clearing in the forest, and under a waning Moon, he makes his way along the track. He remembers his initiation at the Spring Equinox; his love for the Virgin, and their joyful celebration of the Land Marriage at Beltane; he remembers how proud he was of his creative powers at the Midsummer Solstice, and with a pang of sadness, he remembers how he had to face the dark challenger who threatened his Kingdom and his Queen. And finally, he remembers the birth of his son - a joy now turned to sorrow, as the King finds himself once more in the clearing, where waiting at the centre is his son, armed with a spear.

Out of the corner of his eye, the King sees a movement in the shadows, and remembers how he first saw his beloved wife, when she was newly awakened, a young Virgin, and he was the Lord of the Forest. Now his wife hides in the shadows - she wears a black cloak, and covers her face with its hood. The King and his son face each other, and then without a word being spoken, the King draws his sword and they begin to fight. Sword against spear, a mighty battle rages in the clearing. The powers of light and dark are equal, but the powers of darkness are now in the ascendant, and as the night grows on, the King begins to tire. The wasting wound he suffered at the Summer Solstice has never healed, and his powers - like those of the Sun - are waning.

There is a brief pause in the fight: the King and his son look deep into each others' eyes. There flashes between them recognition of the mystery that light and dark are equal: that they are not fighting each other, but that each is fighting himself. For the light and the dark are one and the same, as are the King and his son, and with this realisation, the King joyfully lifts his guard, and is impaled upon the spear as he drives his sword deep into his son's heart. Together they fall dead to the ground, and their blood pours out upon the Earth.

At the edge of the clearing the Queen watches, and as she sees her husband/son die, she sends a great wail echoing through the forest. There, standing in the cave mouth is the Lord of Death and Resurrection, but she cannot see him. For her husband/son/lover has now become the Lord of the Otherworld, and she is still of this world. The waning Moon watches as she tears her hair, and as one possessed, runs through the forest in an agony of grief. For she too saw the mystery, and now she understands that the light and dark are but the same. She knows that her husband/lover/son has passed beyond the veil, and that her creative time is past. For the Queen is now a Witch: the ancient Hag Crone who knows the mysteries of life and death and has walked the path of initiation. In making her journey she has truly found the gods, and knows that behind the wheel of the seasons there is an ancient power. By walking the wheel she has joined with the mystery. She has been a Virgin, a Wife, the Queen, the Mother and the Crone. She has walked the way of the seasons. She has seen the spring, the summer, autumn and winter, and she understands that an ancient truth lies hidden within it all.

Now the Queen stands alone; outcast, feared by those who have yet to walk the Wheel. Her powers are potent, as she haunts the dark forest, seeking for ways to re-unite with her husband/son/lover. At last the time arrives: it is a dark Moon, and the Sun's powers are low. The veil between the worlds is thin. Alone in the forest she makes her way to the clearing, for now she must perform the supreme act of magic. She kindles the ancient Samhain fire, with woods of all the sacred trees.

One for each season, one for each way, one for the night and one for the day, one for her lover and one for her son, one for the serpent and one for her song.

As she raises her arms in invocation a great storm gathers. With a final act of understanding she opens the veil between herself and the gods; she opens the veil of the Otherworld, for she has discovered deep within herself the secret of the mystery. As she parts the veil, the storm breaks: lightning and thunder tear and crack at the ancient night as the trees creak and bend in the wind. For the wild hunt is now upon us as the spirits of the dead are led from the Otherworld by the Horned God. Chaos now reigns in the world for the Mystery is upon us.

To fulfil this mystery, the Crone must embrace the Lord of the Flame, the Lord of Death and Resurrection, and go with him back into the Otherworld. To join with him she must become the Goddess. So of her own free will, she dies the death of true initiation. She enters into the cave, and passes with the Horned Lord back into the depths of the Otherworld. There they join in love as one: the supreme moment of the true Great Rite in which all the mysteries of the male and female; all the mysteries of the light and dark are married together as one. For love has always been the key. It is love that conquers our fear and shows the way to union. For true love is true death, as the individual sense of self is transcended by a vision of the One. As the gods fulfil the mystery of love, the seed of new life is planted deep within the womb of the Great Mother.

And the land sleeps, for the dark time is upon us once again, and the God and Goddess lay in each others arms, deep within the Land, hidden from sight. The Sun quickly wanes day by day, the nights growing longer, the days shorter. Winter grips the land as a cold wind blows through the forest. The darkness seems complete, but those of the Wicca are wise and weep not for they know that the Sun will be reborn through the love of the God and Goddess. Life will not fail - the Sun will return again. And at last the night of the Midwinter Solstice arrives: the longest night of the year, but we know now it is only the darkness that comes before the dawn. As you sit in the darkness, you begin to be aware once more of your everyday surroundings. You feel the floor beneath you, and hear sounds around you. You allow the image of the forest to fade, and allow your consciousness to return once more to the everyday world. Slowly move your arms and legs, gradually stretching and moving every part of your body. When you feel that you have fully returned to your normal state, open your eyes, and stand up.

If you want to make any notes do, but please remember that the Wheel of the Year is an emotional experience, not an academic exercise! And finally, always have something to eat and drink after any activity which uses an altered state of consciousness. This is the most effective and efficient way to "ground", and is vital if participants are travelling home after the working.

The Wheel of the Year pathworking leads through one entire cycle, using one very potent set of images. In a coven, each of these experiences would be explored in ritual form, as one Sabbat leads to another. The guided visualisation is a very good way of providing an overview of the entire cycle, but it is only by exploring each aspect individually that you will be able to penetrate the many mysteries the Wheel contains.

For this reason, we have included in Chapter 7 a set of Festival rituals, which are suitable for complete beginners, as well as more experienced practitioners. You can of course amend them, to take into account the numbers and talents contained within your own group, but it is important to retain the principles that each one represents.

CHAPTER SEVEN

A BOOK OF SHADOWS

A Book of Shadows is a very personal thing. Whilst members of a coven would normally copy out the contents of their initiator's Book of Shadows, no two books are ever alike, for each person changes and adds to the contents, to suit their own needs and interests. Over the past twenty years or so, a number of books about Witchcraft or Wicca have been published, many of which contain the author's own version of a Book of Shadows, or extracts from those used by Gardner and Sanders. It is important to remember that a Book of Shadows (from whatever source) is not holy writ, and is intended to be used as a guide, not an inflexible set of instructions which must be obeyed at all costs!

Books of Shadows are personal documents, and what is important to one person, may be utterly irrelevant to another. If you are a member of a coven, the book used within that coven will normally provide you with the basis of your own. However, your Book of Shadows will grow as you grow. As you learn more, and discover more, you will copy into your own Book of Shadows whatever inspires or interests you. This can be anything from doggerel verse, to recipes for Sabbat Cakes, to a curious bit of folklore, an extract from a novel you have read, to a ritual which you have written - anything at all which is important to you.

In our coven, we continue the practice of our initiates copying whatever they want from our Books of Shadows by hand. This may seem archaic in this day and age, but there are a number of good reasons for the tradition.

Although it is of course far easier to photocopy something, by writing (or typing) it, you are actually reading the text at the same time - very important where magical work is concerned. It also makes sure that you only copy what you really want; no-one is going to spend hours copying out rituals which they never intend to use. Wicca teaches us to focus upon those things which are really important to us, and so copying by hand is all part of the learning process.

Later, you will find that different people will give you rituals, songs, recipes, and so on, and of course you will come across many different things yourself that you would like to keep. You can simply file all these, but it will mean much more to you if you transcribe them by hand into your own Book. We encourage people to use a "springback" type folder for their Book of Shadows, which can easily be reorganised to accommodate new material, and yet does not require holes to be punched in the paper.

Perhaps most importantly, copying the rituals into a special book is an act of magic in itself. Whether you use an elegant script and a fountain pen on parchment, or simply print with a biro on lined paper, the act is the same, and is a very important magical process.

This chapter does not include the standard Gardnerian/Alexandrian rituals, invocations, charges, etc., which have already been published in a number of books. The most complete Book of Shadows of this kind will be found in "The Witches' Way" by Janet and Stewart Farrar (see Appendix A for details). Instead, we have concentrated on the Wheel of the Year, and other magical rituals which are mentioned elsewhere in this book.

Where reference is made in the rituals to tools, cauldrons, and so on, by all means replace these with something else, or omit them entirely if you prefer. They are no more than symbols, and as long as the principles are followed, the tools are very much up to each individual. The words "cakes and wine" are used throughout the rituals, but what you actually use to bless and share at this point is up to you. So too with the "feast", which can be anything from a cup of coffee and a biscuit, to an elaborate 12 course banquet!

The abbreviations HP (High Priest) and HPS (High Priestess) are used to indicate the couple who are leading the ritual. Obviously it is not essential to have a male/female partnership lead the coven, and some covens do not have these offices at all. So, the HP and HPS roles in the rituals may be allocated as necessary within your own group, as long as the general principles are observed.

When any words have to be spoken in ritual, it is essential that they be learnt, not read from a book or crib sheet. There is nothing guaranteed to ruin a good ritual more than having pieces of paper flapping about, or someone stumbling over words they can hardly see in the dark! If you have trouble learning lines, then understand the principle of what you need to say, and make it up on the night. If you cannot speak in ritual (some people find this difficult), then amend the ritual, or write your own, and use actions instead of words. Do try to learn the rituals though; we are following what was essentially an oral tradition, and should at least attempt to make our brains and memory work a little!

The poetry and invocations used in the following rituals come from a variety of sources, some previously published, others appearing for the first time in print. The authors include Julia Phillips, Rufus Harrington and Doreen Valiente, and there are some traditional pieces whose author(s) are unknown. There are also some excerpts from the Gnostic Mass by Aleister Crowley, and a poem by Rudyard Kipling.

Finally, experienced Wiccans will notice that we do not give instructions for invocations to be performed upon a person. This is intentional, as the book is aimed at beginners, and those who do not necessarily work within a traditional coven structure.

Although the year begins with Samhain, it also ends there, and so we begin our Book of Shadows with the Midwinter Solstice; the time of the re-born sun.

MIDWINTER SOLSTICE

Common name: YULE, derived from Anglo-Saxon GIULI. This name was recorded by Bede (?673-735 CE), and was said to incorporate the last month of the old year, and the first month of the new. Anglo-Saxon authority Sir Frank Stedman says that it is, "a name so old, that its meaning is quite uncertain.". (Anglo-Saxon England, OUP, 3rd ed., 1985)

Time of year: the midwinter solstice varies from year to year, but is generally either the 22nd or 23rd of December (northern hemisphere); 21st or 22nd June (southern hemisphere). It is best to check an ephemeris rather than rely upon a diary, as the data in a diary is not always accurate.

Time of ritual: any time on the day of the solstice, although a ritual to mark the moment of the actual re-birth of the sun (i.e., dawn) is a good idea.

Key aspects: The sun; re-birth; beginnings; promise of new life; light returning.

The Winter Solstice Ritual

(This particular ritual was intended for the night before the solstice.)

If outdoors, a clearing in a wood or forest is ideal. If indoors, some holly and ivy or other local greenery should decorate the Temple.

Cast your circle in the usual manner, but with only one white or yellow candle on the altar, so that you are in darkness. We fix a candle to a small log, which is decorated with holly and ivy, rather than use a candlestick - our own version of the Yule Log! Of course out of doors, you would need to place your candle in a jar, which could also be decorated with holly and ivy. Place the cauldron in the centre, with one unlit white candle inside it, and a taper for each member of the coven.

93

The four quarter candles are in their places, but unlit. Have a few pots of sand or earth handy.

HPS says:

"Let us dance for the long year's end, for the sun has set in the west, and we begin the long night of hope."

Coven do a slow dance deosil about the cauldron chanting: Time and death, life and seasons, all must pass, all must change. The dance ends when HPS raises her arms. She or the HP then says:

"This is the night of the Solstice; the Mother Night. Now darkness triumphs, and yet gives way to light. We watch for the dawn, when the Mother again gives birth to the Sun, who is the bringer of hope and the promise of summer."

From now until the sunrise, the coven can tell stories, meditate, or do whatever they feel appropriate at this time. Some covens start the ritual at midnight, so it can be a few hours between this point of the ritual, and the next.

At the first rays of sunrise, the HPS lights the candle in the cauldron and says:

"Behold the mother who brings forth the child!"

(If the ritual is not timed for sunrise, the HPS can simply light the candle in the cauldron as she speaks these words)

Once the cauldron candle is lit, the HP and HPS light the tapers, and the coven members start to move around the circle. Each one is handed a lighted taper, and all chant:

"Power of light and magic free

94

> Eternal power of infinity
> Light of dark and light of day
> Speed the spokes fast on their way."

The quarter candles are lit by designated members of the coven during the chanting and circling, which continues, gaining in speed until the power peaks, and the HPS signifies the end.

The HP and HPS now place their tapers into a pot of sand or earth, and each coven member does likewise. These should be left to burn out naturally (but please be sensible, and place them somewhere safe).

Cakes and Wine

In our coven, we have a tradition at Yule of exchanging gifts. The gift must be home-made, and suitable for either male or female. All of the gifts are wrapped and placed in a large cauldron (not the one which contains the candle!), and after cakes and wine, each person has a "lucky dip" for their present. This is understandably a very popular tradition, and has enabled people who had previously believed themselves totally incapable of making anything, to uncover amazing talents.

The Feast

Close the circle in the usual way (this can be done before the feast, if preferred).

END OF WINTER/BEGINNING OF SPRING

Common names: CANDLEMAS, OIMELC, IMBOLC, BRIGID. Oimelc and Imbolc (or Imbolg) are Celtic names, both meaning "ewe's milk". The name is recorded in the Ulster tale of "The Wooing of Emer by Cu Chulainn", where Emer sets Cu Chulainn a task of going sleepless from "Samhain, when the summer goes to its rest, until

Imbolc when the ewes are milked at spring's beginning; from Imbolc to until Beltine at the summer's beginning and from Beltine to Bron Trogain, earth's sorrowing in Autumn". (quoted in The Pagan Religions of the Ancient British Isles, Dr Ronald Hutton, Basil Blackwell Ltd., 1991).

Candlemas is the name given to the festival by the later Christians, who kept many of the features of the earlier Pagan ceremonies.

You will also hear this Festival called Brigid, as in Ireland, St Brigid's Day falls on 2 February. Brigid is one of the most popular goddesses in Ireland; so popular, that the Christian Church could not remove her from the hearts of the people, so they made her a saint! On the eve of her feast day, young people in Ireland carry an image of Brigid (usually a corn dolly or Brigid Cross) from house to house. In the house where she "rests", she is laid in a bed, and a phallic club placed beside her.

Time of year: unlike the solstices and equinoxes, Imbolc is not connected to a particular astronomical event. As Emer says, it is the time "when the ewes are milked at spring's beginning...". Our ancestors did not have a set date for this, but a time of year. However, when the festival times were recorded by the Christian monks as they transcribed the oral traditions, they were set to a day. As we have all grown up with the Christian calendar being dominant in our society, most Pagans continue to celebrate on the date recorded by the Christians, which is February 2nd in the northern hemisphere. Of course, in the southern hemisphere, end of winter/beginning of spring does not fall during February, and so the date for this festival in the southern hemisphere is August 2nd. In Celtic societies, a festival was usually celebrated on the preceding night, and so Imbolc will often be held on 1st February or August, rather than the 2nd.

Time of ritual: any time, although most Imbolc celebrations are held after sunset.

Key aspects: light (usually represented by many candles); first menstruation for girls; first flowering in the plant world; awakening; animals who hibernate often begin to awaken now; lambs are born; beginning of self-knowledge and self- determination.

The Imbolc Ritual

This particular ritual follows the tradition of honouring Brigid. A corn dolly, dressed in white silk, is placed in a bed (we use a small raffia fruit basket), with a phallic club beside the dolly. The bed can be decorated with snowdrops or crocuses. As an alternative, have a look at the ritual for the Spring Equinox. A suitably amended version of this (focusing upon the awakening one of the female, rather than the male) makes an excellent Imbolc ritual.

The Temple (or outdoor site) should be in darkness, apart from a candle in the centre of the circle. We use the Yule log, which was a part of the Midwinter Solstice ritual. Brigid in her bed should be placed on a small altar, with unlit candles either side of her, and lots of unlit candles in sand pots around the room or site. (We normally have fifty or more candles.) A cauldron should be in the centre of the room, with a jug of water by its side. The cauldron should be empty, except for a small bunch of herbs, tied at the stems. There should be a taper for each member of the coven in a handy place somewhere in the Temple or site.

The Circle is cast in the normal manner. The coven holds hands, and dances in a circle to some suitable music. We sometimes use "Gaudete" by Steeleye Span, but anything which appeals to you, and is relevant for the ritual, is fine. If out of doors, and recorded music is impractical, the coven could sing or chant.

When the music or chant finishes, all remain standing around the cauldron. The HPS picks up the jug of water, and says:

97

"Now behold the icy rivers
Touched by sunlight, turned to blood;
See the waters flowing freely,
Through the gates of land and love."

As she says the third line, the HPS pours the water into the cauldron. She then takes the asperge, and all circle around her chanting the Witches' Rune. As each person passes, they are sprinkled with the water from the cauldron, the bunch of herbs being used as an aspergillus. When the rune finishes, each person takes a taper, and two people who were previously chosen light their tapers from the one lit candle. They approach the altar, and each lights one of the candles either side of Brigid, saying:

"Brigid is come, Brigid is welcome!"

The coven responds by exclaiming:

"Brigid is come, Brigid is welcome!"

The HP says:

"The darkness of winter is passing: the Earth awakens once more from its slumbers; the Virgin walks among us again, and brings Her blessings upon the land and upon our lives."

Everyone now lights their taper from the centre candle, and the HPS says:

"Let the inner light bear fruit in our own lives, even as the Earth bears the first flowers."

Everyone now starts to walk deosil around the Temple, lighting all of the candles that have been placed around the room chanting:

"Thus we banish winter, thus we welcome spring;
Say farewell to what is dead, and greet each living thing."

When all the candles have been lit, and the tapers stuck into pots of sand and left to burn out naturally, the HPS says:

"Welcome Brigid: She of the Golden Hair; Queen of the White Hills, and rider of the White Swan. We give thanks for your three gifts of fire. The first is the flame of creation; of the poet and artist; of the lovers' passion for union with the beloved. The second is the flame of purification and testing, the flame of truth. With this flame all dross and weakness are made clear and cleansed from us, so we become like a true and tested sword. The third is the greatest of all, for it is the healing flame born out of the love that gives all, the maker of peace and harmony."

Cakes and Wine

Feast

Close the circle

It is customary for Brigid's bed to remain in the home for a year, as a guardian and protection. Lighting a candle by the side of Brigid's bed on a regular basis throughout the year is a nice custom. Some people bury the Brigid doll at the following Samhain, which is symbolic of the descent of the Goddess to the Otherworld at this time. Whatever you choose to do, the corn dolly symbolises the Goddess, and should be treated accordingly.

SPRING EQUINOX

Common names: SPRING EQUINOX, EOSTRE. This festival is most commonly called Spring Equinox, but some Pagans have named the festival Eostre, after the Anglo-Saxon Goddess of the spring. We know nothing of Eostre, other than her name, and the fact that Bede says that the Anglo-Saxons named the fourth month of the year after her. Some people have suggested that the name Easter is derived from Eostre, and that the Christian festival of resurrection is akin to the earlier Pagan tradition of the resurrection of the Earth, which occurs during this time of year.

Time of year: at the Spring Equinox, which varies from year to year, but is usually 21st or 22nd March (northern hemisphere) and 23rd or 24th September (southern hemisphere).

Time of ritual: any time, although as this festival celebrates equal light and dark, with light in the ascendant, dawn would be a good time.

Key aspects: day and night are equal; rising sap, leading to leaf burst on trees; plants and trees begin to flower; rite of passage from boyhood to manhood.

The Spring Equinox Ritual

This ritual is designed to awaken the young male aspect that is found within each of us. (It can also be used at Imbolc, with a young woman in the main role.)

Altar and quarter candles lit. Temple decorated with leafy branches (if indoors). Circle cast in the usual manner, with a young male member of the coven blindfold (with four separate blindfolds), at the centre. The rest of the coven should each take the role of an animal of their choice, with four of them to represent the four elements. For example, lion for fire; hawk for air; bull for earth; salmon for water.

The HP says:

"O Child of Yule: I call Thee to tread the path of the Fool.
Of the howling winds and the fire a-kindle;

100

Of the horse's mane and sidle and bridle;
Of the coarse hard rock and the soft silent sea;
A distant memory I would awaken in Thee."

Ha! But you are blind and not yet fit to wear the crown.
If wear it ye would ye must wander around
Until four certain animals ye have found:
Each one will Thee a question ask, T
o answer correctly will be your task!"

The "animals" now start to move around the circle, as the young man tries to catch them, in a game of blind man's buff. As he catches each one of elemental animals, a riddle will be put to him which he must answer correctly: when he does, one blindfold will be removed. The game can continue for as long as you like, but must last until all four riddles have been answered correctly. (The riddles can be as obvious or as difficult as you like, but should pertain to the element of the animal which poses the question.)

When the last blindfold has been removed, the HP will present a sword or wand to arm the young man. (NB: if the ritual is used at Imbolc for a woman, a sword can still be presented, or any other symbol of the woman's awakening power and self-knowledge.) It can be appropriate at this point for either male or female for a new name to be given.

The HP will then light a candle saying:

"We kindle this fire today in the presence of the Mighty Ones
Without jealousy, without envy, without malice,
Without fear of aught beneath the sun save the High Gods.
Be thou a bright flame before us;
Be thou a smooth path beneath us;
Be thou a guiding star above us;
Kindle thou in our hearts within
A flame of love to our neighbours;
To our friends, to our foes, to our kindred all;

To all creatures on the broad earth,
From the lowliest thing that liveth,
To the name that is highest of all."

The young man then leads a dance, to celebrate his passage to manhood.

Cakes and Wine

Feast

Close the circle

BEGINNING OF SUMMER

Common names: BELTANE, BELTAINNE, BELTINE, BELTAIN, BEAL-TINE, BALTEIN. Of all these Celtic names, the most common spelling is Beltane, a Scottish variant used by Sir James Frazer in his monumental study, The Golden Bough. In Wales, the native name for this Festival, the most important of the Welsh year, is Calan Mai.

Readers of Dennis Wheatley novels will also have read of this festival being called Walpurgis Night, which is an English translation of Walpurgisnacht, the eve of the feast day of St. Walpurga, an 8th century Abbess in Germany. St Walpurga's Day is May 1st, and German folklore tells that the on the eve of St Walpurga's day, a witches' sabbath is held on the Brocken in the Hartz Mountains.

Time of year: According to "The Wooing of Emer", Beltane is held, "at the summer's beginning...". In many rural places in the British Isles, Beltane was celebrated once the Hawthorn (or May) had blossomed, hence many of the sayings about bringing May into the house. This has nothing to do with the month, but with the blossom. As with Imbolc, when the Celtic myths were transcribed by the Christian monks, dates were ascribed to the Festivals, and that for Beltane is May 1st (northern hemisphere). However, following the Celtic tradition of the festival being celebrated on the preceding night, Beltane is usually celebrated on 30 April (northern hemisphere). In the southern hemisphere, Beltane is still celebrated at the correct time of year, the beginning of summer, on 31 November.

Time of ritual: it really depends on the type of ritual. Quite often, Beltane rituals incorporate a fair or other gathering, in which case, either a full day, or afternoon, is ideal. If the celebration is more of a coven ritual affair, then whenever is the most suitable time for the ritual you will be using.

Key aspects: the maypole; joining of male and female energies; seed being planted (secondary planting); learning to share; recognising the male and female within; growth; celebration.

The Beltane Ritual

Whether indoors or out, we always have a maypole as part of our Beltane ritual. If out of doors, a tall thin tree can have ribbons tied around the trunk. Indoors, we use a trimmed candlestick pine trunk, which is wedged between the floor and ceiling in our Temple. Ribbons are nailed to the top of the trunk, and a garland of flowers decorates the crown. A couple are chosen as the Hawthorn Queen and Oak King we choose a couple who are already partners, but obviously this will depend upon the people performing the ritual. We make two crowns; one of blossoms and flowers for the Hawthorn Queen, and a crown of oak leaves for the Oak King.

Circle is cast in the usual manner.

All hold hands and circle deosil as the HPS chants:

> "God of the meadow, God of the hill,
> God of the sap and of our true will:
> Thee I invoke as Spring awakes,

103

Thee I invoke as the blossom breaks.
Come young God, come come with the fire,
Lissome and leaping, alive with desire.
Come with the pipe and come with the drum,
With the heartbeat's pounding, come God come!

O seeker of joy, O hunter of pleasure,
Come enter the ring, tread the pagan measure.
Be here in Thy servants, be here in Thy Priests,
Be here in the flesh, and join in the feast!"

The HP then continues with:

"Goddess of Spring, Goddess of Fire,
Goddess of laughter and our desire,
Thee I invoke as Spring awakes,
Thee I invoke as the blossom breaks.

Come young maid, come come with thine power
Fragrant and lovely as a spring flower
Come with thy harp and come with thy song,
With the heatbeat's pounding, come maid come!

O giver of joy, o giver of pleasure,
Come enter the ring, tread the Pagan measure.
Be here in they servants, and in Thy Priestesses,
Be here in the flesh - join our festivities!"

As he says the final line, everyone stops circling and raises their arms.
Then everyone slowly lowers their arms, and lets go of their
neighbours' hands. The group should stay in a circle, but leave a space
between each person for the Hawthorn Queen and Oak King to pass in
and out during their "love chase".

The Hawthorn Queen begins to weave her way in and out of the circle,
and is chased by the Oak King. She keeps herself on the other side of

the circle from him, and they chase each other round and round. As they do, the rest of the group sing the Beltane sing and clap their hands.

Beltane Song:

O do not tell the Priests of our art
For they would call it a sin
But we've been out in the woods all night
A conjurin summer in

And we bring you news by word of mouth
Good news for cattle and corn,
For the sun is coming up in the south
With oak and ash and thorn

Sing oak and ash and thorn my boys
All on a midsummer morn
Surely we sing of no little thing
In oak and ash and thorn

(song is repeated until the King holds the Queen)

The King should eventually capture the Queen through his realisation that hunting her is not the way to her heart! How he expresses this is up to him, but one way would be to call to the Hawthorn Queen, tell her of his love for her, and ask her to wait for him. They embrace and kiss, and then kneel before the altar to receive their crowns. The HP and HPS place the crown of flowers on the Queen's head, and the crown of leaves upon the King's head.

King and Queen now rise, and form with the group a circle about the Maypole. As the music or singing starts, everyone takes a ribbon. The men take a RED ribbon, and the women take a WHITE ribbon. Women face anti-clockwise; men face clockwise, and start moving around the Maypole, going under the first person, the over the second, under the next, and so on. Keep your eye on your own ribbon! Sometimes - depending on the dancers - the ribbons are unwound again, which can be the difficult bit! The dancing continues until the singing or music stops. We like to leave the ribbons wound around the maypole, but this is up to you.

The Hawthorn Queen and Oak King perform cakes and wine, to share their blessings amongst all present.

The Feast

Close the circle

(Suitably amended, this ritual also makes an excellent handfasting)

SUMMER SOLSTICE

Common names: MIDSUMMER or LITHA, which is the Anglo-Saxon name for the sixth and seventh months, and is thought to mean "moon".

Time of year: at the Summer Solstice, which varies from year to year, but is usually 21st or 22nd June (northern hemisphere) and 22nd or 23rd December (southern hemisphere).

Time of ritual: many people celebrate this ritual at mid-day, to honour the sun at its height on the longest day. Others choose dawn, and some sunset. It is very much a matter of personal preference, as long as it fits with the type of ritual you have chosen.

Key aspects: achievement; light; maturity; first glimmer of darkness, often symbolised by a male "challenger".

The Summer Solstice Ritual

This ritual should be performed out of doors, beginning at mid-day.

Each member of the coven should carry a leafy branch, decorated as they like with ribbons, coloured tokens (especially little balls of bright yellow, to symbolise the sun), bells, and anything else which seems appropriate.

One member of the coven male if possible should be nominated to represent the darkness. He should wear a black cloak over black clothes, with a veil across his face. Or, you could use body paint to decorate him instead. He should remain hidden from the coven until his moment to challenge.

Led by the HP, the coven makes a procession to the Temple or working site, all carrying their decorated branches. As they enter, the HP begins to walk in a deosil circle, and everyone follows him, visualising the circle being cast. We would have some "sun" music playing at this point, or would sing a suitable song. When the song or music finishes, everyone stands still, and faces inwards. The HPS takes some consecrated salt-water, and walks around the circle deosil, sprinkling salt-water over each person present.

The HP says:

"O circle of Stars whereof our Father is but the younger brother, marvel beyond imagination, soul of infinite space, before whom Time is ashamed, the mind bewildered, and understanding dark, not unto Thee may we attain, unless Thine image be Love. Therefore by seed and root and stem and bud and leaf and flower and fruit do we invoke Thee."

The coven responds by proclaiming:

"So Mote It Be!"

At this point, a chain or similar dance should take place, with each member of the coven holding aloft their decorated branches, shaking it gently so that the bells ring. (Chain dance: half the coven face one way, half the other, and they weave in and out of each other as they dance around the circle.) Another suitable dance, if you know any of them, is a Morris Dance.

Towards the end of the dance, "darkness" makes his entrance, in as dramatic a manner as possible, bursting into the circle. He should rush towards the dancers, "threatening" them, waving his arms around, and generally giving as good an impression of approaching danger as the person taking the role can portray. The dancers respond by shouting and screaming, and trying to keep him away from them. This goes on for a while, and eventually, all the dancers band together, and as a group, waving their branches before them, they advance upon "darkness" and drive him from the circle.

Once "darkness" is outside the circle, the HP "closes" the gap in the circle which darkness caused, and says:

> "Threaten no more, creature of darkness! I banish you from here!"

Darkness responds by saying:

> "Fool yourself no longer! Darkness is in the world once more, and my time is approaching. Today, you rule, but my time will come!"

Darkness then throws a spear (a stripped wooden branch is ideal) at the HP, striking him on the leg. The HP, drops to his knees as though wounded, and Darkness runs off, laughing, and saying:

> "My time will come!"

The HP stands, but is limping, as he and the HPS make their way to the altar to perform cakes and wine.

Feast

Close the circle.

SUMMER'S END

Common names: LAMMAS, LUGHNASADH, BRON TROGAIN. Lammas is perhaps the most common, being derived from the Anglo-Saxon Hlafmas, or Loafmass, a celebration of the harvest. However, Lughnasadh (Celtic) is also well-known, and was celebrated throughout the ancient Celtic world. In "The Wooing of Emer", this time is called Bron Trogain, but that does not seem to be as widespread as the name Lughnasadh.

Time of year: traditionally, when the harvesting was completed. However, the Christian Church has also adopted this festival, commemorating St Peter's release from prison (as the seed is released from the husk of the corn!), and set the date as August 1st (northern hemisphere). In the southern hemisphere, this time of year falls in February, with the 1st or 2nd being the date when most Pagans celebrate Lammas.

Time of ritual: after sunset, as this festival is concerned with the returning darkness.

Key aspects: reaping; child-birth (Earth bringing forth); second recognition of growing darkness; recognition that things are no longer growing; seed; gathering in, and giving thanks.

The Lammas Ritual

The Temple or working site should be decorated with dried corn or grain stalks, fruits, berries, and nuts. On the altar should be some home-baked bread, and a dish of honey. Traditionally, barley wine or mead is in the chalice for this festival, but wine or beer is also suitable, and any fruit juice.

Circle is cast in the usual manner. The coven join hands, and dance to a suitable song (e.g., John Barleycorn) or chant. When this finishes, the HPS stands before the altar and says:

"Now as the days grow shorter, and the crops have ripened, we give thanks for the good things of the Earth. As time of harvesting draws to its close, may we learn the mysteries of the Earth Mother, and feel Her with us all through this life."

The coven responds by saying:

"So Mote It Be!"

Now each member in turn comes forward, bringing a gift for the Earth, and says:

"Thank you for the good things you have given to me. Thank you for the food in my belly, the water which gives me life, the fire which gives me warmth and light, the air which I breathe, and the Earth which is my home. I give you in return a small gift; a symbol of my love for all the things which you have given to me."

The gift is placed upon the altar, on in the cauldron. Each member in turn comes forward, ending with the HPS and HP, who then continue with cakes and wine. This is a little different to the normal ceremony. The chalice is blessed, and returned to the altar. The bread and honey is blessed by the HPS, which the HP continues to hold. The HPS then picks up the chalice. Each member of the coven then comes forward in turn, takes a piece of bread, and dips it in the honey. They eat this, and then take a sip from the chalice. The HP and HPS do the same, once everyone in the coven has come forward.

Feast

Close the circle

AUTUMN EQUINOX

Common names: AUTUMN EQUINOX, MABON. Autumn (or Fall) Equinox is the most common, although some Pagans have adopted the name Mabon, son of Modron, who appears in the Celtic legend of Culhwch and Olwen. The Anglo-Saxons called this time Halegmonath, which means "holy month", or as Bede translates it, "month of offerings".

Time of year: at the Autumn Equinox, which varies from year to year, but is usually 23rd or 24th September (northern hemisphere), and 21st or 22nd March (southern hemisphere).

Time of ritual: any time, although as this festival celebrates equal light and dark, with dark in the ascendant, dusk would be a good time.

Key aspects: equal night and day; recognition and acceptance of the dark; seeds begin to fall to the ground; trees loose their leaves; plants wither and die.

The Autumn Equinox Ritual

Have one black, and one white (or yellow) candle on the altar. Decorate the Temple with autumn leaves, apples, autumn flowers, etc. The person who played the role of "Darkness" at Lammas should be similarly dressed as on that occasion, and again, be outside of the circle while it is cast. A black cloth, at least three metres by two metres, should be folded and placed by the altar.

Circle is cast in the usual manner. The coven join hands, and walk around slowly chanting:

"Spring, summer, autumn, winter;
All things pass, all things fade, All things die."

As they walk around, the HP is visibly limping.

When the coven finishes, the HPS says:

"Mysterious energy triform, mysterious Matter, in fourfold and sevenfold division; the interplay of which things weave the dance on the Veil of Life upon the Face of Spirit. Death! Term of all that liveth, whose name is inscrutable, be favourable unto us in thine hour!"

The HP stands as an old man, and says:

"You have all pursued my theme, through its winding way around the wheel. A fool sees not the same tree as a wise man sees. In my youth, I did not understand this. Now, as the shadows wrap themselves around my soul, I understand much I did not in my youth. I will leave you shortly. Be not afraid. Watch, and listen, and learn."

The HP calls:

"Darkness! Your time arrives, as you said it would. But this time, I shall invite you into the world; you come as guest, not as intruder."

The HP cuts a gateway in the circle, and Darkness enters. He walks around the circle, standing before each person. He does not threaten, but each person draws back from him. Finally, he stands before the HP and says:

"So old man, we meet at your invitation. Light has need of Darkness, does it? But you were wrong to call me guest; I am come at no-one's bidding but my own. You and I are one and the same; I cannot summon you, no more can you summon me. But if you will join me, we can pass beyond the mystery which is called Life. Alone, you and I are but shadows and reflections; as one, we pass beyond Life itself. What say you?"

The HP responds:

"You ask too much. You ask that I leave this world, my wife, my people. You ask that I forego the beauty of the fertile earth, the fresh breath of air, the warmth of the sun, the eternal sea. It is too much."

Darkness:

"What are those things compared with a journey through the gate of night and day? What are they compared with the Mystery of Life itself?"

HP:

"I am afraid, and yet I will join with you, and travel to the heart of the Mystery."

Darkness and the HP embrace each other, and gently fall to the ground. The HPS covers them both with the black cloth, and then walks around the circle, and extinguishes all of the candles, except for one black candle on the altar. She stands alone at the altar, and blesses the cake and wine saying:

"In death, there is life. Behold the mystery."

Cakes and wine are shared amongst all present in the usual way, although "Darkness" and the HP remain hidden under the shroud.

The HPS leads the coven out of, and away from, the circle, so that the HP and Darkness can come out from under the black cloth, and "re-appear" as ordinary people again.

Feast

Close the circle

BEGINNING OF WINTER

Common names: SAMHAIN, HALLOWE'EN. Hallowe'en is a contraction of All Hallows Eve, the night before All Saints or All Hallows Day in the Christian calendar. When the Christian Church adopted Samhain, they retained many of its features, including being a time to honour and remember those who have died. Samhain and all of the variant spellings, are Celtic. The pronunciation varies depending upon dialect, but is commonly pronounced "Sowain", or "Saveen". The Anglo-Saxons also had a name for this festival, Blotmonath, which means "month of sacrifice", according to Bede, who explains that this is because, "they (the Pagan Anglo-Saxons) devoted to their gods the animals which they were about to kill." This practice of dedicating to the gods stock culled before the onset of winter was also shared by the Celts.

Time of year: the beginning of winter, or as Emer puts it, "Samhain, when the summer goes to its rest...". In the northern hemisphere, this festival is celebrated on October 31st, and in the southern hemisphere, on April 30th.

Time of ritual: after sunset.

Key aspects: honour and remembrance of those who have died; remaining seeds fall to the ground, often helped by high winds; the main planting; the Wild Hunt; journey to the Otherworld; the union of God and Goddess.

The Samhain Ritual

Two black candles upon the altar, which is decorated with bare branches, nuts and seeds. If you have an elder tree, a sprig of elder berries can also be placed on the altar. As you cut the berries, say a "thank you" to the Dark Goddess, for there is a rhyme which says: "Elder be your lady's tree; touch it not or harmed you'll be". If the ritual is out of doors, lay a fire in the centre of the circle, ready for lighting. If indoors, have a cauldron in the centre, containing at least 6 inches of sand, on which are placed half a dozen or so charcoal blocks. If they are good quality, they can be lit before the circle begins, but if the small explosive type, light them just before they are used in the ritual. Have a pot of incense on the altar. The HP stands outside the circle, out of view.

Circle is cast by the HPS alone. Her partner, remember, departed to the Otherworld at the Autumn Equinox.

The coven hold hands, and circle slowly chanting:

> "Come one tonight to the standing stone
> Come one tonight, come honour the Crone
> Come one tonight as the Wild Hunt rides
> Come one tonight at the gathering tide"

The chant continues, and after a few rounds, the HPS lets go of the hand of the person on her right, and turns the circle dance into a spiral. Once the centre of the spiral is reached, it reverses, and the HPS leads everyone back into a circle dance.

The HPS stands before the altar and says:

> "Now is MY time. I am the crone, and darkness is my

power. Now I shall perform the greatest of all magic, and summon back to this world my lover, for without him I am lonely."

She invokes:

"By the flame that burneth bright O Horned One,
We call Thy name into the night, O Ancient One!
Thee we invoke by the moon led sea,
By the standing stone, and the twisted tree.
Thee we invoke where gather Thine own,
By nameless shrine, forgotten and lone.
Come where the round of the dance is trod,
Horn and hoof of the goat foot God!
By moonlit meadow and dusky hill,
When haunted wood is hushed and still,
Come to the charm of the chanted prayer,
As the moon bewitches the midnight air.
Evoke Thy powers that potent bide,
In shining stream and secret tide,
In fiery flame and starlight pale,
In shadowy hosts that ride the gale.
And by the fern brakes, fairy haunted,
Of forests wild and woods enchanted;
Come O come to the heart beats drum,
Come to us who gather below,
When the pale white moon is climbing slow,
Through the stars to the heavens height,
We hear Thy hooves on the wings of night!
As black tree branches shake and sigh,
By joy and terror we know Thee nigh.
We speak the spell Thy power unlocks,
At solstice, sabbat and equinox.
Word of virtue, the veil to rend,
From primal dawn to the wide world's end!

As she says "veil to rend", the HPS opens a gateway in the circle, and the HP enters, as Lord of the Wild Hunt. The HPS tries to catch him, and chases him around the circle, but is unable to grasp him. All the coven members should be moving around as well, as the whole scene should symbolise the Wild Hunt. Eventually, the HPS realises that she cannot catch the Lord of the Wild Hunt, as he has passed beyond this world. She realises that to fulfil the Mystery, she too must choose to pass beyond the world of men and women. She calls out to him:

"I understand! My power does not come from Darkness; but from Darkness and Light; from man and woman; from the Earth and Starry Heavens, and there is no part of me that is not of the gods. I behold the Mystery!"

Everyone stands still, as the HPS approaches the Lord of the Wild Hunt. He walks backwards towards the gateway in the circle, followed by the HPS. As he steps out of the circle, he holds out his hands to the HPS. She reaches beyond the circle, and grabs his hands. They leave together, and perform the GR (symbolic, or actual). One person within the circle closes the gateway behind them.

If the ritual is held out of doors, the central fire is now lit. If indoors, the charcoal blocks are lit (if necessary) and the pot of incense collected from the altar. If out of doors, the coven seat themselves around the fire, and look at the flames; if inside, each person in turn places some incense on the charcoal, and then uses the incense smoke instead of the flames an aid to meditation. This is the point of the ritual where all those who have died are remembered, and thought of with love and honour. When everyone has spent as long as they need in quiet meditation, two people go to the altar and bless the cakes and wine, which are passed around in the usual manner.

After cakes and wine, the HP and HPS rejoin the group for the feast.

Close the circle

A WICCANING

A Wiccaning is a ceremony to welcome a new child. It can also be used to welcome a new pet into the family, for to Wiccans, animals are just as much sacred children of the gods as we are ourselves. First, for a child:

If the parents are performing the ritual alone, they should gather together some of the following items, which are placed in dish, together with a small bag, on the altar:

a piece of wood from a tree, which has special significance to the parents; an ear of wheat, or other grain; a small jar of natural water (not salt); a nut of some kind, still in its shell (hazel, or an acorn, are quite good); a stone; a sea shell; one item to represent the God; one item to represent the Goddess; plus anything else which the parents would like to include.

If there are guests invited to the Wiccaning, then each can be asked to bring a small item which will be blessed and given to the baby. Any such gifts should be placed in the dish with the other items, above.

Circle is cast as usual, with parents and baby inside. If guests are present, they join hands around the family group, and dance to a suitable song or chant. If the parents are alone, they can sing to their child.

The HPS and HP (or mother and father) remain in the centre of the circle, and ask for the blessings of the God and Goddess upon the child. It is best to speak from the heart, but suitable words might be:

> "We ask that you bestow your blessings upon (name), child of (mother and father's name). Guide him/her, watch over him/her, and keep him/her from harm."

Then go to each of the quarters in turn, starting in the East saying:

"Guardians of Air: We ask that you bestow your blessings upon (name), child of (mother and father's name). Guide him/her, watch over him/her, and keep him/her from harm."

(If you have different elemental attributions to different quarters, follow your own tradition).

Then go to Fire, Water and Earth in turn, asking for blessings, etc., in each quarter.

A variation upon this is to replace the four elements with that used within the Celtic tradition, of Land, Sky and Sea. Whichever seems most appropriate to you is the one to use.

The parents now stand before the altar, holding the baby between them. The HPS and HP (or mother and father) take it in turns to pick up one item from the dish, showing each one to the child saying the following, and then placing the item in the small bag:

"Here I give you wood from the (name) tree, that you will know and love the trees, and learn of their wisdom;

Here I give you wheat (or other grain) that you will always have enough to eat;

Here I give you water, taken from the (name) river, that you will always have enough to drink, and will always be able to find water;

Here I give you a seed from a tree (a nut), that you may understand how great things grow from small beginnings, and that you may become as strong and true as a tree;

Here I give you a stone, that you may feel the strength and steadfastness of the earth from which it comes, and that you will understand the power that comes from stillness and silence;

Here I give you a shell, a gift from the eternal sea, and a symbol of eternal life;"

(Parents now give any other items they, or guests, wish to place in the bag)

"Here I give you (item), a symbol of the Goddess, that you will always remember her, and the great love she has for you.

Here I give you (item), a symbol of the God, that you will always remember him, and the great love he has for you."

Tie the bag securely, and then give it to the baby. Most babies will hold tightly onto objects they are given, but if he or she shows any sign of dropping the bag, take it gently, and return it to the altar.

Cakes and wine

Feast

Close the circle.

Wiccaning (or protection) for a Pet:

If a cat or dog, place a collar and identity tag on the altar. If some other kind of pet, place on the altar something which the animal will use.

Circle is cast as usual, with pet inside.

The HPS and HP remain in the centre of the circle, and ask for the blessings of the God and Goddess upon the pet. It is best to speak from the heart, but suitable words might be:

"We ask that you bestow your blessings upon (name of pet). Guide him/her, watch over him/her, and keep him/her from harm."

Then go to each of the quarters in turn, starting in the East saying:

"Guardians of Air: We ask that you bestow your blessings upon (name of pet). Guide him/her, watch over him/her, and keep him/her from harm."

(If you have different elemental attributions to different quarters, follow your own tradition).

Then go to Fire, Water and Earth in turn, asking for blessings, etc., in each quarter.

A variation upon this is to replace the four elements with that used within the Celtic tradition, of Land, Sky and Sea. Whichever seems most appropriate to you is the one to use.

Now take the collar (or other item) from the altar, and bless it, asking for protection for the pet.

Cakes and wine

Feast (including some food for your pet, who will remain in the circle)

Close the circle

A HANDFASTING

The Temple or outdoor site should be decorated with ribbons, flowers, and anything else to symbolise the joyful occasion. A red and white cord (made by the couple, or the HP and HPS) should be on the altar, and a broomstick nearby.

Circle cast in the usual manner, with the bride and groom outside the circle.

All present stand in pairs, leading from the edge of the circle where the couple will enter, towards the altar, and make an archway with their hands. The HPS opens a gateway, and calls the couple to enter through the archway, and stand before the altar. The gateway in the circle is closed behind them.

The HP and HPS welcome them to the circle, and ask:

> "Is it your true will to walk the path together? Do you both sincerely wish to be handfasted?"

The bride and groom confirm that this is their desire.

At this point, it is nice for the HP or HPS to read a poem, or dedication, which the couple have chosen themselves. The HP and HPS may also like to offer words of advice, but remember, this is a handfasting, not a lecture!

The couple then kneel before the altar, and place their right hands together. The HP and HPS wrap the red and white cord around the couple's clasped hands, saying:

> "Bound, but free
> You have chosen to journey together, each supporting the other
> Be ever mindful of the thoughts and happiness of your partner
> Keep sacred the vows you promise to one another
> Seek always Truth, and your partnership will blossom and flourish"

The HP says to the bride:

> "Now repeat after me: I (name), in the presence of the Mighty Ones, give my hand to (bridegroom)...."

122

the remainder of the vow should be decided by the bride and groom, and be in accordance with their own wishes.

The HPS says to the groom:

"Now repeat after me: I (name), in the presence of the Mighty Ones, give my hand to (bride)...."

the remainder of the vow should be decided by the bride and groom, and be in accordance with their own wishes.

After the vows, bride and groom rise, as the HP and HPS bless them in the name of the Goddess and the God, and ask for their protection and guidance.

A broomstick is laid across the centre of the circle, and the couple, still bound, jump over it three times. The cord is then removed, and given to the couple.

The bride and groom now lead a joyful dance around the circle.

Cakes and Wine are performed by the handfasted pair

The Feast

Close the circle.

A REQUIEM

Wiccans believe in reincarnation, and so death, whilst inevitably a sad affair for those left behind, is seen as a stage upon a journey. A requiem therefore is a ritual for the living, not for the dead. Wiccans do not believe that death is the end, and so they do not mourn for those who have departed. However, they do mourn for the sadness which results after separation from a loved one.

Every year, Wiccans remember all those people who have died during the Samhain ritual. But a special ritual to mark the passing of someone with whom you were particularly close often helps to come to terms with the loss.

It is not necessary for the body of the deceased person to be physically present for a Requiem. After all, the spirit is no longer present, and the physical shell will be returned to the Earth, as are all things in time. Keep your altar simple, and decorate it with flowers or foliage which the person you are honouring particularly liked. Use their favourite colours and music (but try to make any music you play joyful, rather than sombre), and place on the altar any items of theirs, or of your own, which remind you of them.

Cast a circle, and then sit before your altar, and simply think about the person for whom you are holding a requiem. In a group, sit in a circle facing inwards. Do NOT invoke the person's name, as this could act to hold them to the earth realm. You wish to honour them, not trap them! Think instead of all the happy times you shared, and then visualise the person at the time you loved them best, and "see" their spirit, at this moment, leave the earth body, and flow upwards. Follow it in your imagination, and watch as the spirit becomes more intangible, and finally is absorbed into the universe. Hear joyful laughter, and allow your own joy to rise, knowing that your loved one has safely passed to the next stage of his or her own journey.

This is not an easy ritual to perform, and care must be taken in a number of ways. It is upsetting, remembering things shared with someone who has just died. Never be afraid or embarrassed to show your grief; it is a very human emotion, and is better released than suppressed. Never try to keep the spirit earth-bound; this is a natural tendency if the person was very close to you, but you must honour the spirit, not the physical shell. Let the spirit go.

Finish as usual with cakes and wine, and if you can, make the feast a celebration that the loved one has gone to the next stage of the journey.

Quite often, you will wish to perform a requiem alone, which is understandable. However, try to avoid ending the ritual feeling depressed, for that is not at all the purpose of the Wiccan Requiem.

SPELLS

Spells come in many forms, but are usually a fairly simple rhyming verse, coupled with a physical focus of some kind. The knot spell which appears elsewhere in this book is a classic example. Others from tradition are:

At the Spring Equinox, a single woman should sit at midnight in front of a mirror. There should be no light, except for one candle on the far side of the room. She should look into the mirror and say:

> "Come lover, come lad
> And make my heart glad.
> For husband I'll have you
> For good or for bad."

Presently, she will see the shadowy reflection of her future husband. Of course this dates from a time when young maidens were anxious to find husbands, and perhaps their hopes of a happy marriage were not as strong as their hopes for any marriage!

If a young woman already had a lover, she would set nuts on the hearthstone of the fire, and say:

> "If you love me pop and fly,
> if not lie there silently."

To banish something, you rub it whilst reciting:

> "What is I see is growing
> What I rub is going."

There are lots of similar rhymes, and any good book of folklore will contain many examples.

RECIPES - FOOD

Books of Shadows often contain favourite sabbat recipes. Here is a selection of recipes, which are suitable for ritual feasts.

Rumbledethumps

Cook potatoes, and then mash them with plenty of butter, seasoned with salt, pepper and nutmeg. Add some lightly cooked cabbage, onions and grated cheese, and mix well. You can either serve this as is, or form into patties, and grill until golden brown.

Coven Pie

Variations upon this basic theme have been a mainstay of many a sabbat feast! Steam as many vegetables, of as many different kinds, as you have to hand.

Put 2 tablespoons of butter, and 2 tablespoons of oil, in a saucepan, and fry chopped onion, capsicum and mushroom until soft. Sprinkle over three tablespoons of flour, and stir briskly for a few moments. Slowly add milk, stirring vigorously to prevent curdling. Continue to add milk, until you have a thickish sauce. Season as desired. Place the cooked vegetables into a large pie dish, and add two cups of cooked chick peas. Pour the sauce over the vegetables, and then cover all with a piecrust. A good alternative to pastry is either mashed potatoes or thinly sliced potatoes, dotted with butter. Bake in a hot oven until pastry is cooked, or the potato topping is browned.

Variations: this is a great dish for vegans, if you replace the butter with vegetable oil or vegan margarine, and use soya milk, coconut cream, or nut cream instead of milk.

Meat and fish eaters can add their preferred choices instead of chick peas. The sauce could also be made into a cheese sauce by adding grated cheese after the milk, and stirring well.

Hommity Pie

Boil (or microwave) some potatoes until they are almost cooked. I scrub the potatoes first, but leave the skins on. Chop into chunks about 1" square. In a saucepan, heat 2 tablespoons of butter, and 2 tablespoons of oil, and cook some sliced onion until it is soft. Add the chopped potatoes, and sufficient grated cheese to form a binding for the mixture. Season as required. Line a flan dish with shortcrust pastry, and pour in the mixture. Bake in a hot oven until the pastry is cooked.

Other good main course dishes include nachos, barbecued vegetables, vegetable curries, and good old jacket potatoes. Avoid choosing anything which needs elaborate preparation, or critical timing at the cooking stage. In Europe, many practising Witches and Wiccans are vegetarian, and as a result, most people prepare vegetarian food for the feast. In Australia and New Zealand, Pagans are less likely to be vegetarian, although it is always worth checking. It can be very embarrassing to turn up with your kilo of dead animal for the feast, and discover that your host and hostess are vegetarian!

Ginger Syllabub

1 pint of double cream rind and juice of one orange 1/2 jar of ginger marmalade or chopped preserved ginger with some of the syrup 1 oz white wine 1 oz brandy 2 ozs ginger wine

Whip the cream until thick, and then gradually add all the other ingredients. Mix well, and refrigerate.

Athol Brose

Beat together 1 pint of double cream, 1 tablespoon of honey and 2

127

tablespoons of whiskey. Chill, then serve in small glasses topped with toasted oatmeal.

Generally, a selection of fresh fruit is an excellent choice for dessert, and a lot healthier than the very rich (but very popular!) desserts mentioned above. Cheese boards are another favourite, and can be as simple or elaborate as you like.

Sabbat Biscuits

(Everyone has their favourite sabbat biscuit recipe. This is one of our favourites)

8oz butter
1lb wholemeal flour
8ozs raw sugar
4 eggs
rind of 1 lemon
chopped roasted hazelnuts or flaked almonds

Rub butter into flour, add sugar and lemon rind. Beat eggs and add. Roll out quite thinly and cut into crescent moon shapes. Brush with beaten egg white and sprinkle with nuts. Bake in a medium oven for 10 minutes.

RECIPES - INCENSE

Loose incense is usually a mixture of one or more of certain gums, resins, herbs and essential oils, all blended together. Small quantities are then placed upon hot charcoal blocks to burn. You can buy ready-made incense, or you can make your own. Incense making is a skill rather like cooking: you often start off by following a recipe, but once you have mastered the basics, you can be as creative as you like.

A few words of advice: any organic substance (other than those with a high water content) will burn, but some definitely smell better than others! Avoid making incenses with a high proportion of dried herbs, leaves, seeds, bark, root or flowers, as these nearly always burn with an acrid smell, no matter which plant you use.

Most incenses work best if you start with a gum base, and then add a small amount of dried herbs or flowers, and mix with essential oil or liquid oleoresin. You really should use a pestle and mortar to combine your ingredients, but if you do not have one, then you can use a glass bowl to mix, using a knife. Avoid plastic, as some oils will eat it away, and like wood or other porous substances, it is very difficult to clean properly. Once made, your incense should be stored in a glass jar, preferably with a bakelite lid.

A few simple recipes follow which can be used in conjunction with the rituals described in this book:

Incense to bring good health:
5 mil Frankincense (Olibanum)
5 drops Orange oil
2 mil Gum Benzoin
2 mil Hyssop
2 drops musk oil (synthetic is
  preferable)

Incense of Mercury:
5 mil Gum Mastic
1" Cinnamon (crushed)
1 mil Gum Benzoin
1.25 mil Blade Mace
10 drops Patchouli oil

Incense of the Sun:

5 mil Frankincense
2 crushed Sunflower Seeds
1.25 mil Honey
1.25 mil Angelica (dried herb)
10 drops Cassia oil

Incense to represent an Illness
5 mil Gum Myrrh
5 drops Cedar oil
2 mil Dragon's Blood
2 mil Wormwood

Incense of Air
15 mil Gum Damar
1" cinnamon stick, crushed
2.5 mil Galbanum
2.5 mil Blade Mace
15 drops Dill Oil
5 drops Patchouli Oil

Incense of Fire
15 mil Frankincense
5 mil Benzoin
6 crushed Sunflower Seeds
2.5 mil Orange Flowers
2.5 mil Honey
15 drops Cassia Oil
10 drops Heliotrope Oil

Incense of Water
10 mils Gum Myrrh
5 mils Gum Damar
5 drops Lemon Oil
5 drops Lotus Oil

Incense of Earth
15 mils Peat Moss
1.25 mils Musk Crystals
4 Balm of Gilead buds
5 drops of Cedarwood Oil
5 drops of Pine Oil
5 drops of Vanilla Oil

Please refer to books listed in Appendix A for further information about incense.

FULL MOON RITUAL

Most Wiccans meet on the night of the Full Moon, and in the circle, will practise their skills, meditate, perform healing, and undertake any other tasks which may have been requested. This can be anything from protection for the environment (or the home), to helping find lost property, to asking the gods for guidance and advice, and just about everything in between. Wiccans are nothing if not adaptable!

The lunar current is important to Wiccans, and they will time the work they have to do in accordance with the waxing and waning of the Moon. Traditionally, the Full Moon is used for scrying, and quite often Wiccan circles will incorporate something of the kind in their Full

Moon circle. The following ritual is something rather different though, and is designed to encourage in newcomers the ability to connect with the energies of the Full Moon. It can only be used on a clear night, as it is important that the Full Moon be seen.

This ritual should take place out of doors. If that it impractical, then an open window which shows the Full Moon is essential. Silver or white altar candles are suitable for the Full Moon, and any white or moon-shaped flowers. Your altar setting should contain, in addition to normal tools, a glass goblet three quarters filled with plain water.

Cast the circle as usual, and dance in a circle, chanting the Witches' Rune, or some other favourite rune or song. As the power is raised, everyone should visualise it as a spiral, leading up towards the Full Moon. When the power peaks, everyone should lift their arms above their head, and imagine a second spiral of power coming back down from the Moon, so that a double helix is formed. The HP or HPS now brings the glass of water to the centre of the circle, and all sit or stand around the glass in such a position so that the reflection of the Full Moon can be seen clearly in the water. The visualisation of a double helix is focused into the reflection of the Moon, and everyone holds this image firmly in their minds. After a period of meditation, the HPS will recite the Charge of the Goddess, as everyone continues to look at the reflection of the Moon. When she finishes, she will take up the goblet, and pour a little to the earth. She will then drink some of the water, and pass the chalice deosil to the person next to her. As each person drinks from the chalice, they visualise the power from the Moon passing into their body. When all present have drunk from the goblet, the remainder is poured out onto the earth.

Cakes and Wine

Feast

Close the Circle

NEW MOON RITUAL

Not all Wiccan covens meet at the time of the New Moon. For those that do, it is an excellent opportunity to begin new projects, start practising a new technique, or help something to grow. An excellent ritual which can be combined with the New Moon is one to cleanse and protect a home, particularly one into which you have just moved.

For this ritual, you do not need to cast a circle, but will need a large chalice of consecrated salt/water, a censer that is easy to carry, and a candle in a jar. If there are at least three of you, one should take the salt/water, one the censer and one the candle, with the others following. If only two of you, one person can carry both censer and candle, and the other the salt/water. If you are on your own, you will have to make three trips!

Consecrate all the elements as usual, and make sure that you have some additional incense to replenish the censer if you have a large house. Begin at the eastern-most entrance to your home, and walking in a deosil direction, go around every single room (even the smallest room!), passing from one room to another. The salt/water goes first, asperging continuously as she/he walks around. The censer follows, and then the candle. Pay particular attention to windows and doors. When you have been to every room, pour some of the salt/water that remains onto your front entrance step, and some onto your back entrance step (if you have one). The remainder should be libated into the garden, but obviously not onto your favourite plant, as the water contains salt!

You have no circle to close, but sharing cakes and wine and a feast is still an excellent way to end the ritual.

MAKING A MAGIC MIRROR

You will often find a reference to a magic mirror, but not instructions how to make one. Various techniques for making magic mirrors are taught in all covens, and it really is quite easy. You will need a clear glass dish, similar to an old- fashioned clock-face. It must be concave (or if you turn it over, convex!), and ideally, of a size that fits comfortably in your hands if you cup them together, palms uppermost. Some mirrors are very much bigger, and are kept on a stand, but for a first attempt, a smaller one (say 5" or 6" inches in diameter) is better. You will also need a spray can of matt black paint (any hardware shop will have this).

Once you have your glass, at the next New Moon, clean it, and wash it in natural water. Then, leave it outside, exposed to the elements, for a full lunar cycle. Obviously, being glass, you have to take some care about its position. Don't put it where someone is likely to stamp on it! On a flower bed, or at the base of a tree, is ideal.

At the next New Moon, bring your glass into the circle, and clean it once again. Now is the time that it is prepared for use. Firstly, cover it with a clean cloth (a silk headscarf is ideal). Show the glass to each of the four quarters, and to the God and Goddess at the centre. As you pass around, you slowly unwrap the mirror saying:

"As I reveal this mirror, I ask that visions be revealed to me in the mirror. Not today, but when I seek within the mirror for answers to my questions."

The next part of the ritual must take place out of doors, or in a very well ventilated room. Place the glass with the convex side uppermost onto some newspaper. In other words, the "dish" side of the glass is face down on the newspaper, with the sphere side uppermost. Now carefully spray the glass, making your movements even. Avoid using too much paint, which will "ripple". Leave the mirror in a safe place for several hours (preferably overnight), and then repeat the painting, in a circle again if possible. We will repeat here that if you paint the disk inside, then the room must be well-ventilated.

Keep the glass safely till the next Full Moon, when it is brought into circle, once again wrapped in its cloth.

Still in its wrapping, show the glass to each of the four quarters, and to the God and Goddess at the centre. Then, carefully unwrap the glass, and as you do so say:

> "Blessings upon this mirror. May the God and Goddess guide my visions, and the elements lend their power."

Now sit comfortably holding your mirror, with the glossy, concave side uppermost, and open yourself to any visions which may come to you. You can meditate for as long as you like, but when you finish, spend some time grounding, as scrying work does lead to altered states of consciousness, and it is important to make sure that you return fully to your your normal conscious state.

Cakes and wine

Feast

Close the circle

Keep your mirror wrapped in a cloth when it is not in use.

MAKING A CORD

Another very simple skill, but one which is used time and time again within a coven. The best materials to use are embroidery or tapestry cotton. Decide upon the colour(s) you want, and buy sufficient cotton for at least seven strands (i.e., seven skeins of thread).

Take the skeins, and unravel the threads, laying them out carefully on the floor, making sure that there are no knots or snags. One person stands at each end of the thread (which can be anything up to 9 metres!) and each picks up all the ends of the cotton their end. Holding this firmly, the two people begin to twist the threads. If each person twists in the opposite direction to his or her partner, the threads spiral together, and form a rope. If this doesn't begin to happen relatively quickly, one of you is twisting the wrong way!

It helps at this point to have a third person, who can periodically test the tension of the cord, and establish when it has been sufficiently wound. If not, one of the two people twisting the thread runs their second hand about a foot along the rope, and then brings their hands together. If the rope between the hands quickly winds into a spiral, the cord is ready for the next stage. Being able to judge this accurately will come with practice.

A third person is a definite advantage for this next stage! If not, have a firm object (e.g., a bannister, or door knob) around which you can loop the cord. The idea is that the two ends must now be brought together whilst the cord remains taut. So, a third person can hold the cord at the centre, and move backwards as the other two walk towards each other. Or, the cord can be looped around something sturdy, and the cord kept taut as one person walks to the other. Once only one person holds the two ends firmly, the other person holds the middle, which now becomes, in effect, another end. Holding the cord about six inches from the fold, this end of the cord is "worked" so that it twists into a thicker rope. The two loose ends are held firmly, and once the entire length of the cord has been twisted into a rope, the loose ends are knotted. Later, you can sew (or "whip") the ends if you would prefer not to have any knots in the cord. Some people like to leave one end uncut (i.e., the end which was the middle), making one end of the cord "male", and the other "female". This is entirely up to you. Another nice variation is to thread beads or other objects into the cord as you wind, or, (a very old tradition) for a handfasting cord, the couple could wind strands of their hair into the cord.

Whether you keep it simple, or try something more elaborate, making a cord is a very magical act, and all the time it is being wound, you should hold its purpose very clear in your mind. You can make cords for healing, for handfastings, wiccanings, protection, planetary or zodiacal purposes and whole host of other things. As with most magical acts, the possibilities are endless.

And now, the rest is up to you! We hope this brief Book of Shadows has provided you with some inspiration, and plenty of ideas. The most important thing to remember is that your Book of Shadows is your personal guidebook on your journey; it is a map and a companion, not a rigid set of rules and regulations!

CHAPTER EIGHT

WICCA AND CHILDREN

We were intrigued one day when a non-Wiccan friend remarked that she found it strange that Wiccans - for all their love of nature and the environment - did not encourage children to participate in their rites. "All the books", she said, "describe rituals for adults: there is nothing for the children."

In some ways this is a very accurate perception. Wicca, as we have explained, is unlike most state religions in that it is a mystery tradition which requires its practitioners to undergo a formal initiation which confers upon them the status of Priest or Priestess. This is not something which is suitable for children; in fact most Wiccans will not initiate anyone under the age of eighteen. An analogy within the Christian church would be to have an officiating Priest aged ten!

Wicca is also rather different to most other religions in that it does not proselytise. The belief is that people must be drawn to Wicca, not have it thrust down their throats, and that applies just as much to the children of Wiccan parents as it does to any other would-be initiate. Wiccan parents will generally ensure that their children are encouraged towards a spiritual awareness of the sanctity of the Earth and knowledge of deity, but will not normally insist that the children follow the Wiccan way if they are not drawn to it. In fact most Wiccan parents are only too happy for their children to learn about all the world's religions, and encourage them to appreciate that there are many paths towards the gods, and all are valid.

However, most Wiccan children do choose to follow their parents' religion, probably because it is one of joy and love, and allows them to develop safely within a caring community of spiritually aware people.

Wiccans consider that children are the most sacred gift that the God and Goddess bestows upon humanity.

And it isn't quite true that there is "nothing for the children". There are some rituals which children attend, and others which are written especially for them. The Wiccaning ritual is our equivalent to the Christian baptism rite, but is different in that it does not dedicate the child to the Wiccan religion. It simply welcomes them, names them, and asks for the protection and guidance of the Goddess and God. Wiccanings are times of great joy, when we celebrate the arrival of a divine soul, and watch the mystery of life unfold before our eyes. There are no traditional "rites of childhood" within Wicca, but many parents have created their own rituals to mark the passage in their child's development through puberty, and to adulthood. These are only performed where the child has asked for them, and can be seen as an indication of the close bonds which normally exist between Wiccan parents and their children.

Wiccans would not normally allow children to be present during other rituals for a number of reasons. A child's mind is a fragile thing which is very easy to damage. It is important that children are allowed to develop without being exposed to pressures which they are ill-equipped to handle. Wiccan rituals, because they are activities engaged in by initiates, generate energies which could be overwhelming to a young mind. This is not always so, but no responsible Wiccan would be prepared to take the risk of causing harm, no matter how slight, particularly to a child. However, most parents hold rituals specifically for their children and these are different. These are family affairs, where the parents know and understand what their children can do, and the rituals do not generate any energy which the child may find difficult to handle.

In fact even non-Wiccan parents engage in magical activities with their children: every time they place candles upon a birthday cake and encourage the child to make a wish as they blow them out! Or when the fairies exchange an old tooth for a coin; or when the Solstice greenwood tree is brought into the house for Yule, hung with shiny symbols to represent the re-born sun, exchanging presents on this greatest of all birth-days; or when children look for chocolate eggs laid by the Easter (Eostre) hare (nowadays more often a bunny!); or have a Hallowe'en party where ghosts, skeletons and goblins from the dark night of the Wild Hunt mingle with witches. All of these activities are magical memories of our Pagan past, which many parents - not just Wiccan ones - help their children to enjoy. However, Wiccan parents are aware of the underlying connection between all these magical moments, and are able to help their children explore the wonder and excitement of that greatest of all mysteries: life itself.

Although children are not generally allowed to participate in Wiccan rites, most parents have special celebrations with their children to mark the turning of the seasons. The following Beltane ritual was used by three children (aged 4, 8 and 10) and their parents, and is an example of the sort of ritual which is appropriate for children. As it took place in Sydney, the orientation is to the southern hemisphere.

A Maypole is set up with a garland of flowers, and red and white ribbons in the centre of the working space. The four quarter candles are ready, but unlit. There are pots of earth for each child, and some seeds for planting, and in the cauldron burns a candle - the Belfire.

Mum and the 4-year old light a taper from the cauldron flame, and then light the eastern candle saying: "Here we do bring light and air in at the east". Each of the other three (the remaining two children and Dad) in turn light their own quarter candle saying: "Here we do bring light and fire in at the north"; "here we do bring light and water in at the west"; "here we do bring light and earth in at the south". All then hold hands, and dance in a circle chanting a rune, or singing a song, which is appropriate for this time of year. Mum and Dad visualise the circle being cast as this is done.

Each person now takes a ribbon, and to a suitable song, the maypole dance begins. Children particularly enjoy this, and you can wind and

139

unwind the ribbons as often as you like.

After the dance, everyone sits in a circle around the cauldron, and Mum starts telling a story; at an interesting point she stops, and each child in turn is then encouraged to continue the story using their own imagination. When the story-telling is finished, each child takes a pot of earth and some seeds to the cauldron and says: "Lord and Lady, we ask you to bless these seeds we plant, that they may grow and be strong and beautiful, as may we all." They plant their seeds, and then carry the pots three times deosil around the circle. On the last pass round, they put the pot on the ground, and then jump over the cauldron and make a wish.

Mum and Dad take the cakes and orange juice to the cauldron, and say:

> "Lord and Lady, bless this food and drink into our bodies,
> bestowing health, wealth, peace and love, and that deep
> joy which is the knowledge of thee".

All share the cake and orange juice, and then the feast is brought into the circle.

Finally, the Lord and Lady are thanked, and the quarter candles blown out as the elemental guardians are bid Hail and Farewell. All hold hands as Mum says: "Merry Meet, Merry Part, and Merry Meet Again. Blessed Be".

This simple ritual is ideal for children. It is one in which they can fully participate, and which allows them to be creative. Planting seeds is a nice way to show children nature at work, and it gives them something other than memories to take away from the ritual.

Also, story-telling is an important skill which most modern people have entirely forgotten. Children love to be told stories, but sadly, as they grow older, they are encouraged to leave such childish pursuits behind them. Wiccans believe that there is nothing childish about telling magical tales, and many adult Wiccans use story-telling in their rituals. Children have marvellous imaginations, and if stimulated instead of discouraged, will be happy to use their creative skills throughout their lives.

When Wiccans and their children celebrate the seasons together, or mark the rites of passage, they are times when families re-affirm the great love which they feel for each other, and for the Earth of which we are all a part. The whole of Wicca is a celebration of life, death, and rebirth. As you walk the Wiccan way, you are affirming your own sacred place within the universe; "...for there is no part of us which is not of the gods".

APPENDIX A

RECOMMENDED BOOK LIST

This list represents a selection of those books which we believe will be of most use to those starting to practise Wicca. They cover a wide range of themes, although we have not listed any which are incompatible with pagan beliefs, or which deal with subjects such as divination, astrology, Qabalah, etc. Also, we have not included any books on the subject of historical witchcraft; if anyone is interested in details of these, write to the authors, enclosing a stamped addressed envelope, and we will be happy to provide a recommended reading list.

The omission of a particular book or author from this list does not imply that such books or authors are rejected. In some cases we may not have read the book in question, and this list includes only those books of which we have personal knowledge.

Incidentally - remember that all of these books have been written by northern hemisphere writers, for northern hemisphere readers! Where describing the Wheel of the Year, or ritual techniques, mention may be made of the differences between northern and southern hemispheres, but southern hemisphere readers are generally going to have to make the necessary adjustment themselves to the practices described.

DRAWING DOWN THE MOON ADLER, MARGOT BEACON PRESS (1979, revised 1986)
An impressive overview of the Neo-Pagan scene in the USA, with some mention of Britain. Includes a look at the Wiccan revival generally, and contains interviews, opinions and philosophies, from many different people within modern Paganism.

TRUE MAGICK AMBER K LLEWELLYN (1990)
A very easy-to-read and sensible guide written by an experienced Wiccan High Priestess. Full of common sense, and helpful hints for making the transition into a Wiccan lifestyle.

FIRST STEPS IN RITUAL ASHCROFT-NOWICKI, DOLORES AQUARIAN (1990 - revised edition)
First published in 1982, this book remains an invaluable guide to those who first start practising ritual of any form. The author is Head of Studies of the Servants of the Light, and in this book passes on much of the practical advice which comes after years of study and teaching.

HEDGEWITCH BETH, RAE HALE (1990)
In the form of letters to two aspiring Witches, the author describes her beliefs and rituals in accordance with the turning of the seasons. A really excellent book; well written and well thought out.

COMPLETE BOOK OF WITCHCRAFT BUCKLAND, RAYMOND LLEWELLYN (1987)
A practical guide which contains a little of everything, and a lot of "how to" for those who want to make their own equipment. Anyone working through this book would get a good grounding in a number of skills.

THE ELEMENTS OF THE DRUID TRADITION CARR-GOMM, PHILIP ELEMENT (1991)
This book is a marvellous overview of the modern Druid movement. The author (Chief of the Order of Bards, Ovates and Druids) covers the philosophy, history, and spiritual inspiration of the movement, and demonstrates Druidry's relevance in today's world.

WICCA - THE OLD RELIGION IN THE NEW AGE CROWLEY, VIVIANNE AQUARIAN (1989)
Excellent introduction to Wicca by an experienced High Priestess, and practising Jungian psychologist. Marvellous discussion about initiation, as well as practical advice about techniques used in Wicca, and inspired chapters about the God and Goddess.

THE TRUTH ABOUT WITCHCRAFT TODAY CUNNINGHAM, SCOTT LLEWELLYN (1988)
Sensible little book, despite the author's confusion about the philosophy of ceremonial magicians. A basic introduction, written in an easy-to-read, informal style. Has a good annotated bibliography.

WICCA - A GUIDE FOR THE SOLITARY PRACTITIONER CUNNINGHAM, SCOTT LLEWELLYN (1990)
Useful practical guide - includes rituals and spells, and the author's version of a Book of Shadows.

THE COMPLETE BOOK OF INCENSE, OILS AND BREWS CUNNINGHAM, SCOTT LLEWELLYN (1989)
A practical guide to the composition and use of incenses, oils and herbal mixtures. Easy-to-read and well laid out, the book contains dozens of recipes, tables of correspondences, and lots of common sense.

OTHER TEMPLES, OTHER GODS DRURY, NEVILLE and TILLETT, GREGORY METHUEN (1980)
A look at the occult scene in Australia in 1980. Some of the people interviewed are still active today, and the book provides an interesting historical perspective to Australian occult practices.

WHAT WITCHES DO FARRAR, STEWART HALES (1991 - originally published 1971)
This book was written after Stewart Farrar's first year as a member of Alex and Maxine Sanders' coven. Describes a traditional Alexandrian coven, often quoting Alex and Maxine, and includes rituals and instructions from the Alexandrian Book of Shadows.

THE WITCHES' WAY FARRAR, JANET AND STEWART HALE (1984)
Subtitled, "Principles, Rituals and Belief of Modern Witchcraft", this is the most complete of the Farrar's books. It includes the initiation rites, clairvoyance, healing, spells, and explains Wiccan philosophy. Concludes with an appendix from Doreen Valiente about Dorothy Clutterbuck, by whom Gerald Gardner claims to have been initiated.
NB: In Australia, Canada and the USA, "The Witches' Way" is often coupled with "Eight Sabbats for Witches" and sold as a set under the title of: "The Witches' Bible Compleat".

THE WITCHES' GODDESS (1987) THE WITCHES' GOD (1989) FARRAR, JANET AND STEWART HALE
Each volume contains a look at different deities; their mythologies, and their relevence to modern Wiccans. Includes rituals, advice on invoking deity, and lists a great many gods and goddesses from around the world.

THE LIFE AND TIMES OF A MODERN WITCH FARRAR, JANET AND STEWART PIATKUS (1987)
Has an excellent fictional chapter which describes the feelings of someone at their first circle. Otherwise, this is a compendium of what modern Wiccans think and feel about their religion. Addresses the questions which most frequently crop up from non-Wiccans.

THE SEA PRIESTESS MOON MAGIC THE GOAT-FOOT GOD THE DEMON LOVER THE WINGED BULL THE SECRETS OF DR TAVERNER FORTUNE, DION AQUARIAN (1989)
The first two of these series of novels by Dion Fortune are of particular interest and inspiration to Wiccans, but all of the books are recommended. The "O Great God Pan" invocation found in Wiccan Books of Shadows was written by Dion Fortune, and appeared in Moon Magic.

WITCHCRAFT TODAY GARDNER, GERALD MAGICKAL CHILDE (1982) (Originally published by Aquarian Press, 1951)
Gerald Gardner's exposition of the Wicca and an explanation of his beliefs. Does not contain any rituals, but a very sensible account of modern Wiccan philosophy. Often referred to by more recent authors.

THE MEANING OF WITCHCRAFT GARDNER, GERALD AQUARIAN (1959)
Similar to the above, but much lengthier, and more detailed. Contains a history of witchcraft and folklore from various texts, and a number of literary references which relate to the worship of the Old Gods.

HIGH MAGIC'S AID SCIRE (GERALD GARDNER) MICHAEL HOUGHTON (1949)
Gardner's novel, which he later admitted includes information given to him from his coven. The illustrations and some of the text are heavily drawn from "The Key of Solomon". Not in print, but second hand copies sometimes available.

TRADITIONAL FOLK REMEDIES HOWARD, MICHAEL CENTURY (1987)
An impressive collection of folk remedies and charms, and a comprehensive herbal. Includes a history of folk healing, with many recipes for common ailments.

INCENSE AND CANDLE BURNING HOWARD, MICHAEL AQUARIAN (1991)
An excellent guide to the use of incense and candles in magical practice by a highly respected

144

practitioner of these arts. Includes details of correspondences.

WITCHCRAFT - A TRADITION RENEWED JONES, EVAN JOHN WITH DOREEN VALIENTE HALE (1990)
An interesting book which describes the philosophy and rituals of the tradition taught by Robert Cochrane, which is quite different to that which Gerald Gardner publicised.

ARADIA: GOSPEL OF THE WITCHES LELAND, CHARLES G WEISER (1974)
Describes the practices of witches in Northern Italy at the turn of the century. The author - an American folklorist - transcribed the rituals, spells, and the folklore, told to him by Maddalena, a Tuscan Witch. Some of this book has found its way into the rituals used in modern Wicca.

PERSUASIONS OF THE WITCH'S CRAFT LUHRMANN, TANYA BLACKWELL (1989)
A sociological study of the phenomena of Witchcraft and magic in 20th century Britain. Not a "how to" book, and written in an academic style. Very interesting for its investigation of the beliefs of modern Wiccans.

HERBCRAFT PURCHON, NERYS and CLARY, DHENU JENNIFER HODDER & STOUGHTON (1990)
A wonderful guide to the cultivation and use of herbs in Australia. In "Getting to know the herbs" the author describes their appearance, their cultivation, their folklore, and their use. There is an extensive section about harvesting and storing herbs; lots of information about healing, as well as advice about using herbs in your normal diet to improve your health. Superbly illustrated, this has to be one of the best books about herbs we have ever seen in either hemisphere.

WEST COUNTRY WICCA RYALL, RHIANNON CAPALL NBANN PUBLISHING (1993)
Well presented book, which has some nice bits of folklore and herbalism. The author claims to come from a family tradition in England's West Country, but in this book she describes a variant form of the Gardnerian and Alexandrian traditions.

THE PRACTICE OF WITCHCRAFT TODAY SKELTON, ROBIN HALE (1992)
The first section of this book deals with answers to questions which commonly occur as people first become interested in Witchcraft. Second two contains rituals and celebrations, with section three providing a great many spells and talismans for any number of purposes. An excellent book for beginner and experienced practitioner alike.

THE SPIRAL DANCE STARHAWK HARPER & ROW (1979)
An inspiring book which contains the author's philosophy about Witchcraft and worship of the Goddess, as well as many chants, exercises and rituals.

THE UNDERWORLD INITIATION STEWART, R J AQUARIAN (1985)
A superb guide to the cycle of transformation and spiritual growth which is embodied within the Western Esoteric tradition. A classic, which Wiccans will find of great interest.

LIVING MAGICAL ARTS BLANDFORD PRESS (1987) and ADVANCED MAGICAL ARTS ELEMENT (1988) STEWART, R J
These companion volumes can be read separately, and describe traditional techniques and practices derived from the Western Esoteric tradition. Both deal with the use of creative

145

imagination, visualisation, and the mediation of divine energy. Many practical exercises and rituals are included, as well as excellent guided visualisations.

MAGICAL TALES AQUARIAN (1990) STEWART, R J
Wicca attempts to re-train its initiates in the now almost-forgotten arts of story- telling. Sadly, there are few who are proficient in this art to pass the tradition along. Bob Stewart is one of those who is adept at this skill, and in this book tells 13 stories which he has written over the last 10 years, and which are drawn from the ancient oral traditions of story telling. He describes the techniques of creating, and telling stories, but most importantly, emphasises the importance of story- telling as an art.

WITCHCRAFT FOR TOMORROW VALIENTE, DOREEN HALE (1978)
This book includes some basic Wiccan philosophy, a bit about Gerald Gardner and the early days of Gardnerian Wicca, and then covers all kinds of things from folklore and history through to modern rituals. It concludes with a Book of Shadows.

AN ABC OF WITCHCRAFT PAST AND PRESENT VALIENTE, DOREEN HALE (1984)
An extensive examination of all aspects of Witchcraft, including spells, folklore, herbalism and literary traditions.

THE REBIRTH OF WITCHCRAFT VALIENTE, DOREEN HALE (1989)
Mainly about the modern movement and the earliest days of the revival of Witchcraft. Perhaps of more interest to those who know something about the history of Gardnerian craft than it is to novices looking for a "how to" book about Wicca. Interesting discussion about the influence that artist Rosaleen Norton had upon British Wicca.

APPENDIX B

Invoking

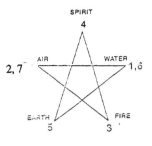	AIR
	WATER
	FIRE
	EARTH

Banishing

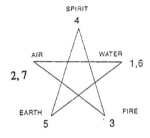

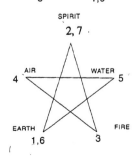

147

APPENDIX C

CONTACTS AND ADDRESSES

If writing to any of the following organisations or publications, please remember to enclose a stamped addressed envelope, or if overseas, at least two IRCs.

PAGAN ALLIANCE (AUSTRALIA) PO Box 47, Carnegie, Victoria 3163

PAGAN ALLIANCE (NEW ZEALAND) 21 Nelson Street, Helensville

PAGAN FEDERATION (EUROPE) BM Box 7097, London WC1N 3XX, England (In Australia: PO Box A486 Sydney South, NSW 2000)

COVENANT OF THE GODDESS (USA) PO Box 1226, Berkeley, CA 94704, USA (In Australia: PO Box 343, Petersham, NSW 2049)

PAGAN MAGAZINES

There are a number of magazines published which are of interest to Pagans and occultists. The following list represents a sample of those which are in publication as this book was written. For subscription rates for each magazine, write to the address shown below, enclosing an sae or IRCs.

AUSTRALIA/NEW ZEALAND

DRAGON'S SONG, PO Box 408, Woden ACT 2606

MAGIC PENTACLE, Box 56-065, Dominion Road, Mt Eden, Auckland 3, NZ

PAGAN TIMES, PO Box A486, Sydney South NSW 2000 (Journal of the PAGAN ALLIANCE)

SHADOWPLAY, PO Box 343, Petersham, NSW 2049

WEB OF WYRD, PO Box A486, Sydney South, NSW 2000